'Drawing on valuable lived experience and deep engagement in research, Dr. Russell writes with conviction to center the voices of undocuBlack students who are too often painfully excluded from spaces of belonging on college campuses across the country. Beginning with her own personal story and bolstered by the similar patterns she found in her interviews with students, the book makes evident the unacceptable gaps in resources and safe spaces. She compellingly calls on all educators and higher education staff to develop policies and practices to better serve these students, first by recognizing their unique needs and contributions. All allies of undocumented students – within and outside of academia – should read this'.

Leisy J. Abrego, *University of California,*
Los Angeles, the United States

'*Amplifying Black Undocumented Student Voices in Higher Education* offers an in-depth and nuanced exploration of the challenges undocuBlack students face. It takes the reader on a journey to understand better the complexities found in the crossroads of anti-Black racism, illegality, and access to educational opportunities in the United States. The stories shared in this cutting-edge work are both heartbreaking and thought-provoking, making it a must-read for anyone interested in equity and justice in higher education'.

Alonso R. Reyna Rivarola, *Salt Lake*
Community College, Salt Lake County,
Utah, the United States

'Felecia Russell's storytelling is nothing short of captivating, and as you read each word of this book, you'll find your heart both shrinking and growing in response to the profound experiences shared within. *Amplifying Black Undocumented Student Voices in Higher Education* is a must-read for scholars, experts, and anyone intrigued by the intricate experiences of Dreamers and undocumented immigrants'.

Gaby Pacheco, *CEO of TheDream.US,*
the United States

'*Amplifying Black Undocumented Student Voices in Higher Education* explores an important gap in the growing literature of undocumented communities in the United States by inserting the voices of undocuBlack students traditionally marginalized in higher education and activist spaces. As a self-identified undocuBlack scholar and higher education practitioner, Russell's work will be critical to the library collections of scholars, community organizers, K-12 educators/administrators, higher education institutions, and policymakers to become undocu competent in practice and advocacy'.

Rafael A. Martínez, *Arizona State*
University, the United States

AMPLIFYING BLACK UNDOCUMENTED STUDENT VOICES IN HIGHER EDUCATION

This book centers a qualitative study exploring the experiences of 15 Black undocumented students and the author's own experiences as a Black DACA (Deferred Action for Childhood Arrivals) recipient, highlighting the invisibility and lack of belonging Black undocumented students face in the undocumented community and the United States at large.

Access and success within higher education for undocumented students cannot be achieved unless those implementing policies understand the full context of the community. Through both an interpretative phenomenological approach and biographical memoir, this volume makes meaning of the experiences of undocuBlack students, a group who do not often see themselves being represented in the immigrant narrative. It argues that without visibility, undocuBlack students are rarely the beneficiaries of advocacy and become targets of overcriminalization. The stories told here examine the intersection of race and identity in determining positioning within society, with the goal of contributing awareness and promoting more inclusive practices among higher education communities.

This text offers an important new perspective for faculty and administrators, policymakers, upper-level undergraduate and graduate students, as well as general readers with an interest in Black and immigrant narratives and the undocumented experience as an academic subject.

Felecia S. Russell is Director of the Higher Ed Immigration Portal at the President's Alliance on Higher Education and Immigration, as well as founder of her own online platform Embracing Undocumented. Dr. Russell identifies as a Jamaican-born, American-raised Black woman.

AMPLIFYING BLACK UNDOCUMENTED STUDENT VOICES IN HIGHER EDUCATION

Felecia S. Russell

Routledge
Taylor & Francis Group

NEW YORK AND LONDON

Designed cover image: Getty Images

First published 2024
by Routledge
605 Third Avenue, New York, NY 10158

and by Routledge
4 Park Square, Milton Park, Abingdon, Oxon, OX14 4RN

Routledge is an imprint of the Taylor & Francis Group, an informa business

ISBN: 978-1-032-58127-9 (hbk)
ISBN: 978-1-032-58150-7 (pbk)
ISBN: 978-1-003-44299-8 (ebk)

DOI: 10.4324/9781003442998

Typeset in Galliard
by Apex CoVantage, LLC

CONTENTS

PREFACE

Oftentimes, I think about the location of my birth and the circumstances under which I was raised. To be where I am from, with the lack of resources that were afforded to me, James Baldwin's words ring loud. He said,

> You were born where you were born and faced the future that you faced because you were Black and for no other reason. The limits of your ambition were, thus, expected to be set forever. You were born into a society which spelled out with brutal clarity, and in as many ways as possible, that you were a worthless human being. You were not expected to aspire to excellence: you were expected to make peace with mediocrity.

From a young age, I would say to myself, 'No matter where you're planted, you are capable of blooming'. I believed wholeheartedly that I was meant to create new traditions, break the generational cycle of dysfunction, and, most importantly, to aspire to excellence. But that aspiration is only true because of the opportunities afforded to me when my mother made the decision to immigrate to America. The doors and the dreams that I imagined walking through seemed possible after I set foot in the flawed land of opportunities. I now had privilege: a liberty to dream big, to imagine a world where I was not expected to make peace with mediocrity but to strive for what my eyes could only imagine.

I am a Jamaican-born, American-raised, Black woman. I am also undocumented. I was born in the small village of Johns Hall in northwest Jamaica. At 11 years old, I left my birthplace and arrived in Inglewood, California, a working class city about 15 miles southwest of downtown Los Angeles.

The streets were different from what I was used to in Jamaica. There were cars everywhere, numerous McDonalds, and a liquor store on every corner.

As a sophomore in high school, I realized that I was an undocumented immigrant. I did not want anyone to know about my status, yet I knew I wanted to go to college, so I eventually decided to disclose my status to my college counselor, Mr. Tovar.[1] He reassured me and told me that I was not alone. He introduced me to a support group on campus for undocumented students. I was excited to attend my first meeting because I hadn't known that there were other students in my situation.

However, on my first day at the student group meeting, I instantly realized that I was the only Black person in the room. I simultaneously felt a lack of belonging and an urge to fit in. One student asked the counselor, 'Why is she here?' He replied, 'She is undocumented too; she is from Jamaica'. I pretended I did not hear the conversation because I was suddenly ashamed that my undocumented-ness did not match their picture of what I should look like (Reyna Rivarola & López, 2021). That student did not mean any harm when she asked the question; she had just never known that Black students could also be undocumented immigrants. I also had never seen any images nor heard any stories about Black undocumented immigrants, so I could understand her perspective. I never went back to those meetings.

Nonetheless, Mr. Tovar was adamant about my success. He told me that I could still attend college even though I could not access federal financial aid as an undocumented student. My only opportunity to receive funding for my education was from private scholarships.

One university did offer me a generous scholarship – California Lutheran University, a private university located in Thousand Oaks, California, just 45 minutes northwest of Inglewood – and with the help of donors, my mother, and other supporters, I made it to college on private scholarships – a privilege not all undocumented immigrant students have.

During my final year at Cal Lutheran, immigrant youth were in the news, fighting for Deferred Action for Childhood Arrivals (DACA), and moved then President Barack Obama to use his executive power to give young immigrants who were brought to this country (as children) an opportunity to be free from deportation and to work in the United States. I remember sitting at home with tears streaming from my eyes because I knew it meant that I could legally work in the country that I considered my home. DACA also meant that I could drive and have proper identification. While DACA was not a complete or permanent solution to the larger social issue of immigration, it was impactful to me.

Once I had completed my undergraduate degree at Cal Lutheran, I had a new dream: I was going to change the world by becoming a lawyer. Unfortunately, I soon realized that without any access to federal aid or graduate loans, I could not afford law school. So, I pivoted and enrolled in a graduate program in Public Policy at Pepperdine University in Malibu, north of Los Angeles. I thought, *If I can't practice law, maybe I will change the laws.* However, through my lived experience as an undocumented student, I fell in love with the idea of providing access to higher education for the marginalized, especially other undocumented students. After all those years fighting for my own education, I realized that I had knowledge to share. Once Trump took office, and deportations dramatically increased, I started thinking about getting other undocuBlack people to college. This sparked my third educational journey: I pursued my Ed.D. at Temple University to study the invisibility of undocuBlack students within the greater undocumented community and within higher education.

What I found confirmed my lived experience: Black undocumented immigrants are often forgotten and invisible. No one thinks we are undocumented. We are disregarded from the narrative and further marginalized within the undocumented community because of our Blackness. This invisibility is linked to an erasure of a group, meaning that Black immigrants are not seen as a group with intersecting identities that influence the way we experience being immigrants. The invisibility of Black immigrants assumes that we are like all other immigrants. More than 619,000 Black undocumented people live in the United States – nearly the population of Las Vegas – but rarely does anyone talk about this community – my community. We are often ignored by the undocumented world, by researchers, policy analysts, professors, politicians, the media, and advocates. Black immigrants are not visible because our stories are not being told. Our stories are not being told because our faces don't represent the U.S. narrative of modern-day undocumented immigration. Our stories are not at the forefront of the struggle for citizenship and recognition. We are not asked to be the faces of campaigns. There are no special scholarships for us. There are no support groups for us. Few know we exist, and the world does not talk about us. But *we* are immigrants as well.

This book is divided into two parts. Part 1, which includes Chapters 1–4, focuses on my personal journey. Part 2 of the book includes Chapters 5–8 and focuses on the experiences of 15 undocuBlack students who I interviewed in 2021.

In Chapter 1, I expand on my personal experience as a Black, undocumented person, providing an extensive account of my journey from Jamaica to America; sharing my experiences as a young person finding out I was undocumented in high school; and describing my college access process and the isolation I navigated as the only Black undocumented student in my high school.

In Chapter 2, I discuss my collegiate experience at California Lutheran University, the barriers I encountered with success, and the challenges I faced at a Predominantly White Institution (PWI).[2] Additionally, I narrate my connection, or lack thereof, to student groups such as the Black Student Union (BSU) and the only DREAMers organization on campus.

Chapter 3 focuses on my graduate school journey, specifically my experiences with access and persistence at Pepperdine University.

Chapter 4 describes my professional trajectory and what led to my third educational journey at Temple University. This chapter culminates with the genesis of this book.

Chapter 5 introduces the 15 stories and provides a personal description of each participant.

In Chapter 6, I address the book's first major theme: sense of belonging. Participants noted that because of their intersecting identities – being Black and undocumented – they often felt a sense of conflict about where they belonged, because they seldom interacted with other Black people in immigrant spaces on campus; the staff in undocumented student resource centers were often Latinx; the programming in those centers was geared toward Latinx students; and the stories and images they saw never represented them. This lack of belonging led to disengagement from the undocumented community and isolation from support systems on campus. I highlight the necessity of community for undocuBlack students.

In Chapter 7, I focus on invisibility among the undocuBlack participants from my dissertation study. First, I position invisibility within the context of American history. Second, I demonstrate the experience for the 15 participants as they navigated their own invisibility. I draw from scholars to corroborate the experiences of non-Latinx students in higher education. I then discuss the participants' reflections on the invisibility they felt in Black spaces on campus, such as BSU (Black Student Union), ASA (African Student Association), and other student organizations focused on supporting Black students. I use the 15 personal stories to bring this theme to life. I conclude this chapter by arguing that while undocuBlack students are having an internal struggle with their immigrant status and their race, they also exist within two broader issues: criminalization and lack of advocacy. I focus on the implications of criminalization and lack of advocacy for undocuBlack immigrants. I contend that Blackness has both direct and indirect ramifications related to political and structural consequences for Black immigrants (Benjamin, 2018). Finally, I argue that because race has always been linked to subjugation in America, there is a connection between Blackness and lack of advocacy.

Chapter 8 serves as the final chapter of Part 2 of the book, and I demonstrate the need to amplify undocuBlack voices and challenge the undocumented and higher education communities to amplify undocuBlack voices. Chapter 8 concludes the book by highlighting undocuBlack organizations and people who are doing important work to support undocuBlack immigrants. Finally, I challenge scholars, policymakers, and higher education practitioners to acknowledge undocuBlack immigrants.

The book closes with an author's note. I provide an update on my current immigrant status, my professional career, and the founding of Embracing Undocumented, my online platform dedicated to serving undocuBlack people.

However, before I transition to Part 1, it is imperative that I provide a brief history of Black immigration in America and discuss the rise of Black immigrants within the United States, their lands of origin, and the issue of undocuBlack immigrants being underrepresented in the immigrant narrative.

Following, I aim to explore the context of higher education and the scarcity of undocuBlack stories within the literature around this group.

Then, I elaborate on the barriers that all undocumented students in higher education face, such as structural, legal, and financial barriers.

Next, it is explained that undocuBlack experiences have been silenced from the literature, but including the voices promotes equity and success of the undocumented community. Following, there is a succinct description of the significance of this book. The preface culminates with a call to handle the stories with care.

At the core of this book is the exploration that undocuBlack immigrants are invisible at the intersection of race and immigration in America. That observation is predicated on the history of the United States, the experiences of Black immigrants in America, and the clear and evident disproportionately negative treatment of Black immigrants within the criminal justice and immigration systems. The 'Black' immigrant, in particular, refers to those who are descendants of the African Diaspora. Black immigrants include Black African, Afro-Asian, Afro-European, Afro-Caribbean, and Afro-Latin American people, among other individuals and groups who are racialized as Black before or upon arrival in the United States.

The story of the United States includes an extensive history of forced migration of Blacks through the slave trade and other means. In the *1619 project*, Nikole Hannah-Jones asserted that the origin story of the United States should be centered in 1619, the original arrival date of enslaved Africans to America. While this centering is controversial within the academy, I also point to that date as an origin for African slaves in America. More than 10 million African slaves were taken from Africa and unwillingly brought to America; over 300,000 of them landed in America through the slave trade (Eltis, 2001). It was not until the early 1800s when Black immigrants voluntarily migrated from Africa (Gregory & Halter, 1995).

Another movement that increased Black immigrants' migration to the United States was the tropical fruit trade among the United States, the

Caribbean, and Latin America, which created a push and pull factor for Black migrants (Hamilton, 2020; Palmer, 1974, 1995). The Black people who were transporting fruits from the Caribbean and Latin America created an entry to the United States for Black immigrants (Palmer, 1995).

During the era of the Civil Rights Movement, the 1965 INA (Immigration and Nationality Act) curtailed lawful immigration pathways from the Western Hemisphere, and it expanded Black immigration to the United States from other parts of the world. Subsequently, the Black immigrant population within the United States began to expand over the following years. There has been a significant increase in Black immigration to the United States. The majority of Black immigrants in the United States are naturalized citizens (56 %), followed by Green Card holders/LPR (29%), and 2% are on nonimmigrant visas (U.S. Census Bureau, 2021).

In 1980, Black immigrants represented 3.1% of the immigrant population in the United States. In 2020, it was estimated that there were more than 40 million immigrants living in the United States (Budiman, 2020). Of that number, Black immigrants represent about 4.2% of immigrants residing in the United States (Budiman, 2020). In 2021, it was estimated that over 9% of the immigrant population reported their race as Black (Lacarte, 2022).

Additionally, the Black immigrant population in the United States is diverse, representing many different countries. Jamaica represents the largest number of immigrants with a percentage of 17%, Haiti 16%, Nigeria 8%, and Ethiopia 6% (Lacarte, 2022). However, while the Black immigrant population comes from a variety of origin countries, they concentrate in certain areas within the United States, such as New York, Miami, DC, and Boston (Lacarte, 2022).

Nonetheless, while there is a presence of documented Black immigrants in the United States, there are also those who are undocumented, residing in the country without legal documentation, referred to in this book as undocuBlack.

UndocuBlack Immigrants

The term 'undocuBlack' was created by the UndocuBlack Network, an organization founded in 2016 to support those who are Black and undocumented. According to the Migration Policy Institute (MPI), in 2021, there were over 45.3 million immigrants living in the United States; of that number, 11 million are undocumented, representing about 23% of the U.S. immigrant population (2021). Additionally, of the undocumented population, 12% are Black (U.S. Census Bureau, 2021). Of the Black undocumented population, 3% are from the Caribbean, and another 3% are from Africa (Lacarte, 2022).

However, while undocuBlack immigrants are present within the United States, they are often ignored by scholars, practitioners, and policymakers and are rarely included in the immigration narrative. Scholars have argued that this erasure and abandonment are partly because of racism and xenophobia (Patler, 2014). Similarly, Benjamin (2018) contended that undocuBlack immigrants are invisible, vulnerable, and marginalized within the undocumented community because of their Blackness. Furthermore, according to Dancy et al. (2018), anti-Blackness is a main point of the undocuBlack experience. As a result of the anti-Blackness and racism experienced by this group, they are overcriminalized within the immigration system and are twice as likely to be held in deportation proceedings than their non-Black counterparts (Meitzenheimer, 2020; Morgan-Trostle et al., 2016). BAJI (2018) reports that Black immigrants represent 20% of immigrants facing deportation compared to only 10% for all other immigrant groups. In 2020, undocumented Black Haitian immigrants alone accounted for 29% of those detained in immigration customs (RAICES, 2020). Furthermore, the average immigration bond for Haitians from 2018 to 2020 was $16,170, compared to $10,500 for other immigrant counterparts (RAICES, 2020). Moreover, undocuBlack immigrants are six times more likely to be sent to solitary confinement while in U.S. Immigration and Customs Enforcement (ICE) detention centers, even though they make up 4% of all immigrants in ICE detention centers (Franco et al., 2020). These discrepancies speak to the disparate harsher outcomes compared to other immigrant populations. Additionally, undocuBlack immigrants are subject to the effects of racialized policing, as Black people are more likely to be stopped and detained for 'traffic' stops (Jones, 2018). They are also affected by mass incarceration, which severely affects Black Americans. It is clear that Black undocumented people face extremely delicate situations as they navigate residing and living in the United States. The experience is even more precarious for undocuBlack students within higher education.

Contextualizing Undocumented Students Within Higher Education

Undocumented students are resilient and diligent people who were brought to the United States as children and grew up in America without documentation. Many of them are no longer children and are now college students. According to a 2023 report by the American Immigration Council (AIC) and the Presidents' Alliance on Higher Education and Immigration (PAHEI), there were over 408,000 undocumented students enrolled in U.S. colleges and universities in 2021. This number demonstrates a 4.2% decrease from the 427,000 enrolled in 2019. This decline should be of concern but can point to the COVID-19 pandemic, low enrollment rates within higher education over the last few years, and the constant legal battles of Deferred Action for Childhood Arrivals (DACA).

While the current decrease in enrollment points to the aforementioned issues, undocumented students still face other significant barriers to higher education regardless of their race and ethnicity. This issue is extremely important because undocumented students need access to higher education in order to eventually earn a college degree. Higher education serves as a primary vehicle of social mobility in the United States. Beyond that, without a college degree, individuals are more likely to be unemployed and/or lack the opportunities for advancement in the workplace that a college graduate would have.

There are policies in place that affect undocumented students' access and success within higher education. One of the policies that affect undocumented students came out of the 1982 court ruling in *Plyer v. Doe*, which declared that states could not deny undocumented students' access to public K-12 education in the United States because of their immigration status; however, that right to access did not extend to postsecondary education. Other federal policies have also shaped access to higher education for undocumented students. For instance, the 1996 Personal Responsibility and Work Opportunity Reconciliation Act (PRWORA) 'bars the provision of "state and local public benefits" for non-qualified "aliens" unless the state passes an affirmative law making them explicitly eligible, including "postsecondary benefits."'[3] This policy made it impossible for undocumented immigrants to receive federal public benefits, including funding for postsecondary education. Without access to federal aid, undocumented students are limited in their access to higher education because of the continued rising cost of higher education. Another federal policy that affects undocumented students is the Illegal Immigrant Reform and Immigrant Responsibility Act of 1996 (IIRA) Section 505, 'bars states from providing "postsecondary education benefits" to those who are "not lawfully present" based on in-state residency unless all citizens of the United States are eligible for those benefits regardless of state residency'.[4] This policy stated that undocumented immigrants were not eligible for postsecondary in-state tuition rates in the United States. As a result of those two federal policies, certain states created their own in-state tuition policies for undocumented students, while others have put in place more prohibitive policies, and others have ignored the issues.

According to the Higher Ed Immigration Portal (2023), as of August 2023, undocumented students have access to in-state tuition in 24 states and DC: Arizona, California, Colorado, Connecticut, District of Columbia, Florida, Kansas, Kentucky, Hawaii, Illinois, Maryland, Massachusetts,

Minnesota, Nebraska, Nevada, New Jersey, New Mexico, New York, Oklahoma, Oregon, Rhode Island, Texas, Utah, Virginia, and Washington. Additionally, of the 24 states, 18 states and DC also provide undocumented students with access to state financial aid: California, Colorado, Connecticut, District of Columbia, Hawaii, Illinois, Maryland, Massachusetts, Minnesota, Nevada, New Jersey, New Mexico, New York, Oregon, Rhode Island, Texas, Utah, Virginia, and Washington. Furthermore, four states provide undocumented students with access to in-state tuition in some but not all universities. Those states are Delaware, Iowa, Michigan, and Pennsylvania. Additionally, five states provide access to in-state tuition only to DACA recipients (Arkansas, Idaho, Maine, Mississippi, and Ohio); eight states and Puerto Rico, nine states do not have known policies (Alaska, Louisiana, Montana, North Dakota, Puerto Rico, South Dakota, Vermont, West Virginia, and Wyoming); and nine states actively block access to in-state tuition for undocumented students (Alabama, Georgia, Indiana, Missouri, New Hampshire, North Carolina, South Carolina, Tennessee, and Wisconsin), including three states which prevent undocumented students from enrolling in all or some public colleges. Those three states are Alabama, Georgia, and South Carolina.[5]

While certain states are moving in the right direction with financial aid policies, there are still broader policies that shape access for undocumented students, such as DACA. In 2012, DACA, an executive order, was issued by former President Barack Obama. To qualify for DACA, an individual:

Was under the age of 31 as of June 15, 2012;
  Came to the United States before turning 16;
  Has continuously resided in the United States since June 15, 2007;
  Was physically present in the United States on June 15, 2012, and at the time of making a request for DACA;
  Is currently in school, has graduated or obtained a certificate of completion from high school, has obtained a GED, or is an honorably discharged veteran; and
  Has not been convicted of a felony, significant misdemeanor, three or more other misdemeanors, or does not otherwise pose a threat to national security or public safety.

(Migration Policy Institute, 2013, pp. 1–2)

Under DACA, undocumented immigrants who met these criteria were granted two-year deferment from deportation, two-year renewable work permits, and social security numbers (Perez, 2014). The program has been instrumental in creating access to higher education for many undocumented immigrants. However, as of 2021, only 141,000 students are DACA-eligible, compared to the 181,000 estimated in 2019 (Batalova & Feldblum, 2023). This decline is due to the constant legal battles with DACA and the impending threat that the policy will most likely end.[6]

In 2022, TheDream.US and Golden Door Scholars released a report noting the impact of DACA. Both organizations surveyed over 600,000 DACA recipients. They found that over 94% of DACA recipients are employed and contribute over 9.4 billion in taxes each year (TheDream.US and Golden Door Scholars, 2022). DACA contributed to undocumented immigrants' access to jobs, internships, study abroad programs, and financial aid opportunities. According to Professor Roberto G. Gonzales (2016), after DACA, undocumented immigrants were able to access jobs, and over 60% of them did so. Additionally, the work authorization that DACA-mented[7] immigrants now had access to also incentivized those who were enrolled in higher education institutions to focus on coursework and complete their degrees (Hsin & Ortega, 2018). Furthermore, more than 78% of DACA recipients reported that DACA made it easier for them to pay for school (Patler & Cabrera, 2015). Additionally, DACAmented students felt increased feelings of safety on college campuses (Gonzales et al., 2018). Therefore, it is evident that DACA provided many positive benefits to undocumented students and their access to higher education.

However, undocumented students still face additional challenges to success while being enrolled in higher education institutions. Undocumented students experience difficulty trusting faculty and staff (Contreras, 2009; Perez, 2010); a lack of physical safe spaces on campuses (Cisneros et al., 2022); and extreme mental health challenges such as anger, anxiety, and depression as it relates to their undocumented status (Conger & Chellman, 2013; Gonzales, 2013). In response, it is essential to provide undocumented students with faculty and staff who can effectively support them; they are in need of allies (Chen & Rhoads, 2016). Research suggests that positive relationships between students and faculty/staff create motivation and support for undocumented students (Contreras, 2009; Gonzales, 2013; Perez, 2010). It is crucial that colleges and universities provide students with faculty and staff who are informed about immigration and the issues facing the undocumented students they serve. Undocumented students also need physical safe spaces on college campuses. Those physical structures on campus are spaces for undocumented students and their families to obtain support (Cisneros et al., 2022). In many ways, students go to these spaces to connect with other students like themselves. The support of peers is very helpful and meaningful for undocumented students and can contribute positively to their successful completion of college (Gonzales et al., 2016; Huber & Malagon, 2007). Existing research proves that colleges and universities should provide a safe campus climate that is welcoming and supportive and provides undocumented students with the resources to be able to navigate higher education.

It is relevant to note that the literature around undocumented students' access to and success in higher education is mainly focused on Latinx undocumented students. However, undocumented students are not all the same, and non-Latinx students face additional challenges within higher education (Huber & Malagon, 2007). Therefore, in the following section, I attempt to provide a brief context on undocuBlack students within higher education and the unique experiences they wrestle with because of race and immigrant status.

Exploring UndocuBlack Students and Higher Education

Because the literature on undocuBlack students within higher education is limited, it is necessary to draw on the history of Black Americans, Black international students, and Black immigrants. Access to higher education in the United States has always been linked to race, and racism has penetrated the fabric of America, leaving Black people with often insurmountable barriers. In fact, Black native students were not able to access institutions of higher education in the United States until after the 1830s (Lewis, 2004). This is important to mention because it demonstrates the entrenched difficulties that Black people navigate as they seek to access higher education. Furthermore, once Black Americans could access higher education institutions within the United States, they were only allowed to attend segregated schools. It was not until 1968 that Black students started enrolling at non-Historically Black Colleges and Universities (HBCUs) and were present at Predominantly White Institutions (PWIs) (Willie & Cunnigen, 1981). Scholars have aimed to understand those experiences, and certain studies indicate that the barriers for Black students on college campuses are related to socioeconomic challenges, discrimination, internalized identity development issues, and stereotypes on white campuses (Constantine et al., 2002; Fordham & Ogbu, 1986; Fries-Britt & Turner, 2001; Ogbu, 2004; Harper, 2009; Harper et al., 2018); those barriers are similar to the ones that undocumented Black students experience. However, there is a constant one-sided narrative that groups all Black students together, and many scholars have critiqued this limitation within the literature (e.g., Dowd & Bensimon, 2015; Harper, 2009, 2015; Yosso, 2005; Yosso et al., 2009).

The experiences of Black American natives and Black immigrant students are similar, yet distinct because of immigrant status (Kim, 2014). However, while those experiences are drastically different and varied, they provide insight into the experiences of undocuBlack students. In 2015, Griffin and McIntosh conducted a study to explore the experiences of Black immigrant students and their engagement on college campuses. They found that since Black immigrant students had multiple identities, they needed peer interactions and wanted to be around others who shared similar experiences as their own. Their findings align with the work of other scholars who purport that the identity of Black students plays a role in engagement on college campuses (Harper, 2015; Museus, 2008).

UndocuBlack students and their experiences are nonexistent within the higher education literature. In 2021, undocuBlack students accounted for 13.8% of the undocumented student population and about 5.7% of DACA-eligible postsecondary students (American Immigration Council & PAHEI, 2023). However, the higher education literature fails to include oppression and its impact on undocuBlack students (Reyna Rivarola, 2017).

UndocuBlack students experience additional barriers to higher education because of their race and immigrant status, and, according to Russell and Reyna Rivarola (2023), they are rendered invisible. This results in the isolation of undocuBlack students among undocumented students within higher education and contributes to the absence of literature about this group. Not discussing undocumented Black students leads to the invisibility of this group, and it perpetuates the narrative about undocumented students 'looking' or 'existing' in only one form, namely the Latinx description.

However, in the last few years, certain scholars have attempted to shed light on other groups within the undocumented community, such as Asian undocumented immigrant (undocuAsian) and Queer undocumented immigrant (undocuQueer) college students (Buenavista, 2016; Dao, 2017; Cisneros, 2018; Cisneros & Bracho, 2019). There have also been studies conducted to understand how Undocumented Student Resource Centers (USRCs) serve undocumented students on college campuses (Cisneros & Reyna Rivarola, 2020). The aforementioned studies are diversifying the literature on undocumented students and shedding light on the continuous gaps within the research.

More recently, scholars have studied undocuBlack immigrant lives broadly (Benjamin, 2018; Meitzenheimer, 2020) and undocuBlack college students specifically (Hall, 2022). In Meitzenheimer's study, the experiences of undocuBlack women and how they traverse or wrestle with gender, race, and immigrant status are explored through the framework lens of Patricia Hill Collins' (1990) 'Black Feminist Thought'. The findings from Meitzenheimer's study demonstrate that undocuBlack women have remained resilient even without the support they need and the silencing of their stories.

Benjamin (2018) demonstrated that undocuBlack students contend with immigrant status and anti-Blackness within the undocumented community and found that undocumented Black people navigate not only being Black but also being undocumented and the additional barriers related to both salient identities. According to Benjamin (2018),

> Black undocumented people have different experiences from the [non-Black] Latinx population in regard to racial profiling, criminalization, educational attainment, and access to jobs, and Black immigrants are resisting marginalization and exercising agency by advocating for their own incorporation into mainstream immigrant rights organizations.
>
> *(p. 14)*

Another recent study that explored the experiences of undocumented Black students is Hall's (2022) study, which showed that undocuBlack students encounter a sense of deletion and erasure from other students, staff, administration, and faculty. Her study emphasizes the need for undocumented Black students' experiences to be explored.

Taken together, three major themes run through the existing literature. First, all undocumented students, regardless of race or ethnicity, face a shared set of common institutional, structural, and legal barriers to higher education. Second, undocumented Black students experience additional barriers that are associated with criminalization, invisibility, and marginalization within the undocumented community as a result of their Blackness. Finally, while I was able to draw from literature on Black American natives, Black international students, and Black immigrants, there was an overall lack of diversity on non-Latinx undocumented students within the literature on undocumented students. Therefore, it is my goal to contribute to scholars', practitioners', and policymakers' understanding of the undocuBlack experience.

Significance

This book centers on my own personal and lived experiences as a Black undocumented immigrant with DACA as well as on a qualitative study conducted in 2021–2022 of the experiences of 15 undocuBlack college students. The study highlights the invisibility and lack of belonging that Black undocumented students face in the undocumented community and the United States at large.

My own experiences navigating the education system have motivated my efforts to bring visibility to undocuBlack immigrants. Therefore, this book positions undocumented Black students at the center of the research and demands visibility and resources for this group.

The matter of invisibility is significant for many reasons. One, if undocuBlack immigrants remain invisible, it is likely that they will continue to be disproportionately affected by deportation. Two, if undocuBlack immigrants stay unseen, they won't be beneficiaries of the resources designed to support the undocumented community. Third, without understanding the experiences of this group, policymakers and higher education professionals cannot provide resources and access to higher education for undocuBlack students.

Awareness and understanding of the undocuBlack immigrant experiences will aid in effectively supporting Black immigrants. Therefore, this book is a scholarly advance that seeks to promote the stories of undocuBlack students and center their lived experiences. This is timely and important, given that so much of the existing literature on undocumented students has largely minimized or erased Black undocumented college students. My goal is not to change the face of immigration but to include undocuBlack faces in an expanded conversation. I am asking for the conversation to be smarter, more nuanced, more inclusive, and more aware.

UndocuBlack stories are special, as they are often untold. I hope you will handle these stories with care.

Notes

1. The stories that are told in this chapter are from my perspective and could be interpreted differently by others. To protect the identity of my family and friends, all names used in this chapter are pseudonyms.
2. California Lutheran University is now an HSI (Hispanic Serving Institution).
3. Personal Responsibility and Work Opportunity Reconciliation Act, H.R.3734, 104th Cong. § 401–423 (1996).
4. Illegal Immigration Reform and Immigrant Responsibility Act, H.R. 2202, 104th Cong., § 505 (1996).
5. The Higher Education Immigration Portal continually updates the facts on tuition and financial aid equity for undocumented students.
6. On September 13, 2023, District Court Judge Hanen ruled that the DACA policy is unlawful, a disappointing ruling that continues to affect the lives of many DACA recipients.
7. Those who have DACA status are often referred to as DACAmented.

References

American Immigration Council & PAHEI. (2023, August 8). *Undocumented students in higher education.* Presidents' Alliance on Higher Education and Immigration. Retrieved from www.higheredimmigrationportal.org/research/undocumented-students-in-higher-education-updated-march-2021/.

Batalova, J., & Feldblum, M. (2023). *Investing in the future: Higher Ed should give greater focus to growing immigrant-origin student population.* Migration Policy Institute. Retrieved from https://www.presidentsalliance.org/the-future-higher-ed-growing-immigrant-origin-student-population.

Benjamin, T. (2018). *Black removal and invisibility: At the intersections of race and citizenship in the 21st century* [Doctoral dissertation, University of Maryland]. UMD Theses and Dissertations. Retrieved from https://drum.lib.umd.edu/handle/1903/21260.

Budiman, A. (2020, August 20). *Key findings about U.S. immigrants.* Pew Research Center. Retrieved from www.pewresearch.org/fact-tank/2020/08/20/key-findings-about-u-s-immigrants/.

Buenavista, T. (2016). Model (undocumented) minorities and "illegal" immigrants: Centering Asian Americans and US carcerality in undocumented student discourse. *Race Ethnicity and Education, 21*(1), 78–91. https://doi.org/10.1080/13613324.2016.1248823

Chen, A. C., & Rhoads, R. A. (2016). Undocumented student allies and transformative resistance: An ethnographic case study. *The Review of Higher Education, 39*(4), 515–542. https://doi.org/10.1353/rhe.2016.0033.

Cisneros, J. (2018). Working with the complexity and refusing to simplify: Undocuqueer meaning making at the intersection of LGBTQ and immigrant rights discourses. *Journal of Homosexuality, 65*(11), 1415–1434. https://doi.org/10.1080/00918369.2017.1380988

Cisneros, J., & Bracho, C. (2019). *Coming out* of the *shadows* and the *closet*: Visibility schemas among undocuqueer immigrants. *Journal of Homosexuality, 66*(6), 715–734. https://doi.org/10.1080/00918369.2017.1423221

Cisneros, J., & Reyna Rivarola, A. R. (2020). Undocumented student resource centers. *Journal of College Student Development, 61*(5), 658–662. https://doi.org/10.1353/csd.2020.0064

Cisneros, J., Valdivia, D., Reyna Rivarola, A. R., & Russell, F. (2022). "I'm here to fight along with you": Undocumented student resource centers creating possibilities. *Journal of Diversity in Higher Education, 15*(5), 607–616. https://doi.org/10.1037/dhe0000355

Conger, D., & Chellman, C. (2013). Undocumented college students in the United States: In-state tuition not enough to ensure four-year degree completion. *Education Finance and Policy, 8*(3), 364–377. https://doi.org/10.1162/EDFP_a_00101

Constantine, M., Robinson, J., Wilton, L., & Caldwell, L. (2002). Collective self-esteem and perceived social support as predictors of cultural congruity among Black and Latino college students. *College Student Development, 43*(3)

Contreras, F. (2009). Sin papeles y rompiendo barreras: Latino students and the challenges of persisting in college. *Harvard Educational Review, 79*, 610–632.

Dancy, T. E., Edwards, K. T., & Earl Davis, J. (2018). Historically White universities and plantation politics: Anti-blackness and higher education in the Black Lives Matter Era. *Urban Education, 53*(2), 176–195. https://doi.org/10.1177/0042085918754328

Dao, L. (2017). Out and Asian: How undocu/DACAmented Asian Americans and Pacific Islander youth navigate dual liminality in the immigrant rights movement. *Societies, 7*(3), 17. https://doi.org/10.3390/soc7030017

Dowd, A. C., & Bensimon, E. M. (2015). *Engaging the race question: Accountability and equity in U.S. higher education.* Teachers College Press.

Eltis, D. (2001). The volume and structure of the transatlantic slave trade: A reassessment. *The William and Mary Quarterly, 58*(1), 17. https://doi.org/10.2307/2674417

Fordham, S., & Ogbu, J. U. (1986). Black students' school success: Coping with the burden of acting White? *The Urban Review, 18*(3), 176–206. https://doi.org/10.1007/bf01112192

Franco, K., Patler, C., & Reiter, K. (2020). Punishing status and the punishment status quo: Solitary confinement in U.S. immigration prisons, 2013–2017. *Punishment & Society, 24*(2), 170–195. https://doi.org/10.1177/1462474520967804

Fries-Britt, S. L., & Turner, B. (2001). Facing stereotypes: A case study of Black students on a White campus. *Journal of College Student Development, 42*(5), 420–429.

Gonzales, R. G. (2016). *Lives in limbo: Undocumented and coming of age in America*. University of California Press.

Gonzales, R. G., Ellis, B., Redon-Garcia, S. A., & Brant, K. (2018). (Un)authorized transitions: Illegality, DACA, and the life course. *Research in Human Development*, 1–16. https://doi.org/10.1080/15427609.2018.1502543.

Gonzales, R. G., Roth, B., Brant, K., Lee, J., & Valdivia, C. (2016). *DACA at year three: Challenges and opportunities in assessing education and employment*. American Immigration Council.

Gonzales, R. G., Suárez-Orozco, C., & Dedios-Sanguineti, M. C. (2013). No place to belong: Contextualizing concepts of mental health among undocumented immigrant youth in the United States. *American Behavioral Scientist, 57*, 1174–1199.

Gregory, S., & Halter, M. (1995). Between race and ethnicity: Cape Verdean American immigrants, 1860–1965. *Ethnohistory, 42*(3), 556. https://doi.org/10.2307/483240

Hall, K. (2022). Undocumented Black students and hermeneutical injustice: Higher education's role in leaving them out of the undocumented conversation. *Journal of First-Generation Student Success, 2*(3), 143–160. https://doi.org/10.1080/26906015.2022.2115327

Hamilton, T. (2020). Black immigrants and the changing portrait of Black America. *Annual Review of Sociology, 46*(1), 295–313.

Hannah-Jones, N. (2019, August 18). The 1619 project. *The New York Times Magazine*.

Harper, S. R. (2009). Niggers no more: A critical race counternarrative on black male student achievement at predominantly white colleges and Universities. *International Journal of Qualitative Studies in Education, 22*(6), 697–712. https://doi.org/10.1080/09518390903333889

Harper, S. R. (2015). Black male college achievers and resistant responses to racist stereotypes at predominantly white colleges and universities. *Harvard Educational Review, 85*, 646–674.

Harper, S. R., Smith, E. J., & Davis, C. H. (2018). A critical race case analysis of Black undergraduate student success at an urban university. *Urban Education, 53*(1), 3–25. https://doi.org/10.1177/0042085916668956

Hsin, A., & Ortega, F. (2018, June 25). *The effects of deferred action for childhood arrivals on the educational outcomes of undocumented students*. Retrieved from https://link.springer.com/article/10.1007/s13524-018-0691-6.

Huber, P., & Malagon, C. (2007). Silenced struggles: The experiences of Latina and Latino undocumented college students in California. *The Nevada Journal, 7*, 841–861.

Illegal Immigration Reform and Immigrant Responsibility Act, H.R. 2202, 104th Cong., § 505 (1996).

Jones, A. (2018, October 12). *Police stops are still marred by racial discrimination, new data shows: Prison policy initiative*. Perma.cc. Retrieved from https://perma.cc/TR86-QGMQ.

Kim, E. (2014). Bicultural socialization experiences of Black immigrant students at a predominantly white institution. *The Journal of Negro Education, 83*(4), 580. https://doi.org/10.7709/jnegroeducation.83.4.0580

Lacarte, V. (2022). (rep.). *Black Immigrants in the United States face hurdles, but outcomes vary by city.* Migration Policy Institute. Retrieved August 21, 2023, from www.migrationpolicy.org/article/black-immigrants-united-states-hurdles-outcomes-top-cities.

Lewis, E. (2004). Why history remains a factor in the search for racial equality. In P. Gurin, J. Lehman, & E. Lewis (Eds.), *Defending diversity: Affirmative action at the University of Michigan* (pp. 17–59). University of Michigan.

Meitzenheimer, B. (2020). *"Know that we exist": Storytelling as self-making for undocu Black students* [Master's thesis, University of California, Los Angeles]. UCLA Electronic Theses and Dissertations. Retrieved from https://escholarship.org/uc/item/7bm6367f.

Migration Policy Institute. (2013). *Deferred action for childhood arrivals at the one year mark: A profile of currently eligible youth and applicants.*

Morgan-Trostle, M., Zheng, K., & Lipscombe, C. (2016). *The state of Black immigrants, part II: Black immigrants in the mass incarceration system.* Black Alliance for Just Immigration and NYU School of Law Immigrant Rights Clinic.

Museus, S. D. (2008). The role of ethnic student organizations in fostering African American and Asian American students' cultural adjustment and membership at predominantly White institutions. *Journal of College Student Development, 49,* 568–586.

Ogbu, J. U. (2004). Collective identity and the burden of "acting White" in Black history, community, and education. *The Urban Review, 36,* 1–35.

Palmer, R. W. (1974). A decade of west Indian migration to the United States, 1962–1972: An economic analysis. *Social and Economic Studies, 23*(4), 571–587.

Palmer, R. W. (1995). *Pilgrims from the sun: West Indian migration to America.* Twayne Publishers.

Patler, C. (2014). Racialized "illegality": The convergence of race and legal status among Black, Latino, and Asian American undocumented young adults. In V. Carty, R. Luévano, & T. Woldemikael (Eds.), *Scholars and Southern California immigrants in dialogue: New conversations in public sociology* (pp. 93–113). Lexington Books.

Patler, C., & Cabrera, A. (2015). *From undocumented to DACAmented: Impacts of the Deferred Action for Childhood Arrivals (DACA) program.* UCLA: The Institute for Research on Labor and Employment. Retrieved from http://escholarship.org/uc/item/3060d4z3.

Perez, W. (2010). Higher education access for undocumented students: Recommendations for counseling professionals. *Journal of College Admission, 206,* 32–35.

Perez, Z. (2014). *How DACA has improved the lives of undocumented young people–center for American progress.* Center for American Progress. Retrieved February 11, 2021, from www.americanprogress.org/issues/immigration/reports/2014/11/19/101868/how-daca-has-improved-the-lives-of-undocumented-young-people/.

Personal Responsibility and Work Opportunity Reconciliation Act, H.R.3734, 104th Cong. § 401–423 (1996).

RAICES. (2020). *Black immigrant lives are under attack.* The Refugee and Immigrant Center for Education and Legal Services. Retrieved from www.raicestexas.org/2020/07/22/black-immigrant-lives-are-under-attack/.

Reyna Rivarola, A. R. (2017). "Undocumented" ways of navigating complex sociopolitical realities in higher education: A critical race counterstory. *Journal of Critical Scholarship on Higher Education and Student Affairs, 3*(1), 101–125.

Reyna Rivarola, A. R., & López, G. (2021). Moscas, metiches, and methodologies: Exploring power, subjectivity, and voice when researching the undocumented.

International Journal of Qualitative Studies in Education, 34(8), 733–745. https://doi.org/10.1080/09518398.2021.1930262

Russell, F. S., & Reyna Rivarola, A. R. (2023). *What does it mean to be Undocu Black? Exploring the double invisibility of Black undocumented immigrant students in U.S. colleges and universities. New directions in higher education. State demographics data–US.* migrationpolicy.org. Retrieved July 1, 2023, from www.migrationpolicy.org/data/state-profiles/state/demographics/US.

TheDream.US and Golden Door Scholars. (2022). (rep.). *New survey of DACA college graduates underscores essential need for dreamers' legislative protections this year.* Retrieved August 21, 2023, from www.thedream.us/wp-content/uploads/2022/11/TheDreamUS-GDS-Alumni_Survey_Report_2022-FINAL.pdf.

U.S. Census Bureau. (2021). 2020 American community survey. *U.S. state policies on DACA & undocumented students: Higher Ed immigration portal.* Presidents' Alliance. Retrieved August 18, 2023, from www.higheredimmigrationportal.org/states/.

U.S. State Policies on DACA & Undocumented Students: Higher Ed Immigration Portal. (2023, August 18). *Presidents' alliance.* Retrieved from https://www.higheredimmigrationportal.org/states/

Willie, C., & Cunnigen, D. (1981). Black students in higher education: A review of studies, 1965–1980. *Annual Review of Sociology, 7*(1), 177–198. https://doi.org/10.1146/annurev.so.07.080181.001141

Yosso, T. J. (2005). Whose culture has capital? A critical race theory discussion of community cultural wealth. *Race Ethnicity and Education, 8,* 69–91.

Yosso, T. J., Smith, W. A., Ceja, M., & Solórzano, D. G. (2009). Critical race theory, racial microaggressions, and campus racial climate for Latina/o undergraduates. *Harvard Educational Review, 79,* 659–690.

ACKNOWLEDGMENTS

To my mother, thank you for making the decision to migrate to America in hopes of providing a better life for your family. Because of you, I had the opportunities that only in America one can have. I love your hustle, grit, and determination to survive.

I am eternally grateful for my community. My high school counselors, Mr. Jorge Torres and Ms. Judy Grood, thank you for believing in me. Without your guidance, I would have never made it to Cal Lutheran. I hope all undocumented students have counselors like you.

Thank you to the Chaney family, the Howie family, and the Ward family. I am grateful for my chosen family. I appreciate your love, support, and encouragement over the years.

Wayne, your generous spirit and unwavering support is a continued motivation in my life. You have always believed in me, and even though we are vastly different, we are so much alike in many ways, and I am pleased in more ways than one to have you as a best friend.

Hannah, in particular was generous with her time, reading multiple drafts of this book, adding her own suggestions and details and helping me make the book as well-written as possible. You have made my life richer in a myriad of ways. Thank you, best friend.

To my first group of friends I met when I first arrived in America: Melanie, Anise, Jasmine, Julian, Raneisha, Ebony, Ariana, and Clarissa. While you all don't know this, you all unintentionally kept me focused on my studies. Thank you for embracing my Jamaican culture and for never making me feel like I did not belong. I mean, there was this one time where Julie said I should know all the lines from Martin and that I had been in America for too long to not know (but, she meant well). To this day, I am most comfortable in this friend setting. To new friends, Alain, Kia, Taylor, Crystal, Jorden, and many others, your support means the most.

Kendra and Kia, you both believed in me, invested in me, challenged me, and supported me. If only every young professional could have supervisors like you, the world would be a better place. To Kia in particular, I appreciate your continued support with proofreading emails, providing recommendations, and our friendship. I love your spirit and your love for Jamaican food, music, and culture.

Dr. Marichal and Dr. Thomas – my two favorite professors at Cal Lutheran – I am so glad to now call you both friends and thought-partners. I appreciate your care for me as a young student, and now I value our friendship.

Miriam Feldblum – you gave me an opportunity at the Presidents Alliance. Not to mention you provided your time in reviewing the preface of this book for me. Your belief in me is appreciated.

Professor Davis – thank you for saying to me, 'You are going to write a book about this topic one day'. You said it so confidently and casually, but I could sense the belief in your eyes. Because of you, I went forth and wrote this book. Thank you for your support.

Shamora and Alrick – I am proud of you both for going to college and for continuing to break generational cycles of poverty and dysfunction. A special shout out to all my other siblings and my nieces and nephews.

Finally, I am forever grateful to the 15 participants who were brave in sharing their stories with me. Because of them, this book is possible. It is my hope that their stories will inspire us not only to tell more undocuBlack stories but also to move beyond stories and implement real change at the institutional and local levels.

AUTHOR'S NOTE

We all balance intersecting identities, whether those identities are queer and female, Black and queer, or undocumented and Black. Our identities influence and impact our lives in major ways. For me, as a Black woman, ostensibly, I understand that the moment I walk in any room, I am seen as such. Being Black comes with its own baggage and stereotypes. Essentially, my Blackness influences the way people see me. Conversely, as an undocumented person, it is not always obvious that I hold this identity. My undocumented status is not always detectable, which has its benefits. However, being undocumented has sizable effects on my opportunities, such as my inability to vote in national, state, or local elections; my inability to travel freely to other countries; and many more. While being Black is obviously visible, my undocumented status is not, but it has a great impact on the way I navigate the world. As a Black person, I can be profiled because of my race, which could then lead to immigration inquiries as I navigate the world with a driver's license that has a renewable two-year limit. Therefore, I live in the crosshairs of both identities. The participants in the study also navigated these positions.

Some scholars argue that race is a master status, such as Hughes (1945), who contends that Blackness is wrapped up in a system of racial stratification in the United States, which dictates that race is the more dominant identity. Hughes defines master status as the identity that greatly impacts your life once compounded with other identities. However, other scholars argue that even when intersecting identities are at play, immigrant status serves as a master status (Gonzales & Burciaga, 2018; Terriquez, 2015). Valdez and Golash-Boza (2020) assert that an undocumented status, when placed next to belonging, race, or class, is not a master status. Enriquez (2017) argues that undocumented status serves as a 'final straw', not a master status, because, when accompanied with other marginalizing identities, it affects educational outcomes for students (p. 1527). Again, it is crucial to note that the scholars who argue that undocumented status is a master status have mostly centered the Latinx experience. Therefore, the nuanced identities that would influence this discussion are largely missing from the analysis.

However, as a Black person and an undocumented person, I argue that race is a master status for undocuBlack people. I align with Hughes (1945), who purports that '[being Black] tends to overpower, in most crucial situations, any other characteristics that may run counter to it' (p. 357). However, after my analysis of the conversations that I had with the undocuBlack participants, it was clear that while being Black impacted their collegiate experiences in seemingly obvious ways, such as discrimination, microaggressions, and stereotypes, none of those issues significantly or explicitly denied them access to opportunities. However, their undocumented status denied them access to community, federal financial aid, internships, and other opportunities that their peers could access. Ultimately, both identities impact their visibility and belonging. This discussion around the impact of invisibility and sense of belonging demonstrates the complex intricacies of race when compounded with an undocumented status and challenges us to reconsider how we think about salient identities.

At the intersection of race and immigration in America is the undocuBlack experience. The undocuBlack college student position is often overlooked and overshadowed by the dominant perspective: the Latinx experience. Specifically, the disregard for undocuBlack student experiences is rooted in racism and anti-Blackness. To belabor, the Latinx perspective represents over two-thirds of the undocumented experience, which signifies the importance and focus on that group. Nonetheless, the centering of only one narrative has consequences for other nuanced experiences, such as the undocuBlack immigrant narrative, which results in overcriminalization and lack of advocacy for this group. I hope that this book will prompt continued conversations around discussions of master status, sense of belonging for undocuBlack students, the invisibility that undocuBlack students face, and the limiting effects of those without DACA.

Embracing Undocumented

When I was a freshman in college, one of my mentors would often ask me, 'How are you going to change the world?' It is a big question. How am I going to change the world? I did not know. And as an undocumented college student, I barely knew how to survive. As a graduate student, I had no direction. However, once I got into the professional world, I continued to climb the ladder of success. By society's standards, I was successful, and even by my own standards, I had made it. But, there was always a pull to answer the question: *How am I going to change the world?*

In 2020, my mentor's question was on the top of my mind. Like many people, the COVID-19 pandemic pushed me to reflect, to contemplate, and to answer tough questions. My mentor's question began making sense. He wanted to know what I would do for others. In 2020, instead of asking myself, 'How can I change the world?' I made it more manageable and started asking myself, 'How can I do something important today?' How will my success help others?

I started Embracing Undocumented in 2020 out of necessity. I could not find stories about undocuBlack people. With all of my intersecting and complex identities, I felt invisible, and I knew there was something I had to do about it.

I also had a desire to give back to the undocumented community, but I did not always have the capacity to do it. For a long time, I was still figuring out how to survive. As you figure out how to survive, you rarely have the capacity to help others. However, in 2020, I found that I had both capacity and desire.

So, I invested in myself and created a template for the work I wanted to do. It manifested into Embracing Undocumented,[1] an online platform that focuses on two areas: sharing the stories of undocuBlack people and connecting young undocumented people to mentors in their field.

My first goal at Embracing Undocumented is to bring visibility to undocuBlack people through narratives. As you know from reading this book, the undocuBlack narrative is often ignored. Furthermore, because undocuBlack immigrants are not usually involved in studies about undocumented people or students' experiences, our stories are often excluded from the conversation, and, as a result, we are not advocated for. Consequently, we are left without scholarships and access to information and resources aimed at serving the undocumented community. Furthermore, we experience discrimination on campus because of our race, as well as isolation, and lack of support from faculty, staff, peers, and even the undocumented community. Because of this lived experience, I want to bring our voices to the table. Therefore, at Embracing Undocumented, I hope to uplift our voices by sharing my story and the stories of others.

The second initiative is to connect young undocumented people to mentors in their field. One of the great blessings of my life as an undocumented person has been my access to a multitude of mentors. As early as I can remember, I had a mentor. I had personal, academic, professional, and spiritual mentors. These were regular people – my high school college counselor, a pastor, a college administrator, my best friend – who were there for me in minor and major ways. They listened to me cry about how unfair the world was to the marginalized and the minoritized. They encouraged my passion to be the first in my family to graduate from college. They wrote me recommendation letters and introduced me to their networks. They opened up a world that was closed to people like me. That's why providing mentorship is one of the main goals of Embracing Undocumented.

I also started a scholarship for undocumented students at California Lutheran University. Creating a scholarship was a way for me to give back to the community in a tangible way. Scholarships carried me through my bachelor's, master's, and doctorate programs. Without them, I wouldn't be writing this book, so I wanted to pay it back. No matter how hard I worked, if there were no opportunities, I wouldn't have both the capacity and the desire to do this work today.

Now, at 32 years old, I can look back and speak to the importance of paying it forward, but at 18 years old, it was about how to survive. Without capacity *and* desire, it is hard to give back. You might have one and not the other. But when you have both, what do you plan to do with it? How do you plan to contribute to the world? To your community? That's how Embracing Undocumented came to be. I am leaving all the doors behind me open for the next generation – and I keep looking back, to ensure I stretch my hands so others can hold on to it, climb to where I am, and even surpass me.

So, if you are a high school or college student, undocumented or otherwise, focus on giving to yourself, and in due time, both capacity and desire will spark and you will know how you want to contribute to the world.

Within the next few years, I hope to take Embracing Undocumented to the next level as a nonprofit organization with a mission to humanize the undocumented population through stories, conversations, and research. In the meantime, I hope you will share this book with others and have discussions about how we move the undocuBlack community forward. I hope you will pay attention to the anti-Black racism that is rampant, partner with undocuBlack and Black-led organizations to promote the visibility of the Black experience, and work to limit the detrimental policies that aim to criminalize and exclude Black immigrants. Remember, anywhere we are planted, we are capable of blooming.

Note

1. https://embracingundocumented.com/

References

Enriquez, L. (2017). A "master status" or the "final straw"? Assessing the role of immigration status in Latino undocumented youths' pathways out of school. *Journal of Ethnic and Migration Studies*, *43*(9), 1526–1543. https://doi.org/10.1080/1369183x.2016.1235483

Felecia Russell. Embracing Undocumented with Felecia Russell. (2022, February 6). Retrieved from https://embracingundocumented.com/.

Gonzales, R. G., & Burciaga, E. M. (2018). Undocumented youth and local contours of inequality. In B. Schneider (Eds.), *Handbook of the sociology of education in the 21st century: Handbooks of sociology and social research*. Springer. https://doi.org/10.1007/978-3-319-76694-2_7

Hughes, E. (1945). Dilemmas and contradictions of status. *American Journal of Sociology*, *50*(5), 353–359. https://doi.org/10.1086/219652

Terriquez, V. (2015). Dreams delayed: Barriers to degree completion among undocumented community college students. *Journal of Ethnic and Migration Studies*, *41*, 1302–1323.

Valdez, Z., & Golash-Boza, T. (2020). Master status or intersectional identity? Undocumented students' sense of belonging on a college campus. *Identities*, *27*(4), 481–499.

PART - 1

1

THE AMERICAN DREAM

My mother (affectionately known as 'Mommy'), a fair-skinned, reserved, no-nonsense woman, was born in Jamaica. She was raised by her grandmother with barely any resources. She never graduated high school. In hopes of creating her own life, she fell in love with her first partner, with whom she had three children. My oldest brother, Grinnell, had dark skin and brown eyes and was extremely resourceful. I never spent much time with him because he was 13 years my senior. Kelly, my oldest sister, was tall and adventurous. Oakley, my older brother and my mother's third child, was short, had a lisp, and loved to play soccer. Mommy's relationship with her first partner was tumultuous, often physically abusive. She left that relationship to start a new one with my father.

Unbeknownst to her, she was unaware of her pregnancy before my father immigrated to America to make a better life for himself. She lost contact with my father and was then left to raise four children on her own. I had a big head, small eyes, and rarely cried, so I was told.

A few months after my birth, I went to live with my grandmother.

Grandma was born sometime in 1938, but she is not sure of the exact date. There were times when she celebrated her birthday in December and other times when she celebrated in January. Grandma had very dark skin, a jerry curl, and a very distinct voice. She had 11 children of her own. I lived with her in the small town of Johns Hall. In that house, two of her children still lived with her. I was the fourth addition to the home.

Johns Hall is a poverty-ridden village that was filled with poorly built homes, rivers, and a few local stores scattered throughout the neighborhood. The house that we lived in was built by my grandmother's last husband, and

DOI: 10.4324/9781003442998-2

it was made of board and zinc, with a poorly covered outside bathroom. There was a big hole in the backyard that was designated as the restroom. I never quite understood how it worked, because there was never any smell coming from the shed, but it had been holding feces for more than 60 years. Our house was painted pink and had three bedrooms and a veranda. It was one of the brightest houses in the neighborhood. Our house was not the sturdiest or the safest, but we made it work. When it rained, we prepared by placing pans and pots throughout the house in case of leaks or flooding. While our house was not the best, my grandmother and mother made sure I had food to eat and a safe place to rest my head at night.

Every day, I had to walk to a river that was about half a mile from our house in order to gather water so that I could take a shower or so that my grandmother could cook. I would walk for 20 minutes at a time to fill up buckets and bring them back to the house. It was fun when other children in the neighborhood were doing it too, but if I had to make the trip on my own, which happened often, I hated it; walking on my own turned it from an adventure into a chore. It was moments like those that made me realize that we were poor.

Living with my grandmother was very structured. She was a Seventh Day Adventist and a devout one. We went to church every Saturday even when it was pouring rain. I could not go outside and play on Fridays or Saturdays because it would be disrespectful of the Sabbath day.

I didn't realize how confined I felt until I saw my mother and my siblings around the village. My mother lived in the same village but on the outskirts. I yearned to be with her. There were times when I would go to her house on Sundays so she could comb my hair and give me money for lunch throughout the week. All of my siblings lived with her, including my younger brother Abe who was born one year after me, and I just did not understand why I could not live with her as well. In Jamaican culture, it is not foreign for children to live with their grandmothers, but the feeling of loneliness and otherness would linger for years into adulthood.

When I was about six years old, my mother came to visit my grandmother, and I overheard them talking about an opportunity that Mommy was getting to go to America. My mother and grandmother sat on the veranda in the two pink chairs that had been fixtures for as long as I had lived in the house; the chairs were old, but they were strong. The veranda was my grandmother's favorite place, and whenever she had visitors, they would join her on the veranda. My grandmother had her most troubling and exciting conversations on that veranda and in those chairs. And on this day, it was no different. She listened to my mom, who asked her if she could look after my younger brother while she went off to America. My mom was very adamant that the opportunity would provide her with the resources to take care of her five children and even support my grandmother. My grandmother agreed. My other three siblings were old enough to be on their own.

Abe came to live with me and grandma, and I was excited because I had been the only child living in the house, and I wanted another child there with me. I did not know him very well other than knowing he was my brother; the only time I was around him was on Sundays when I went to spend time with my mother. Before Abe came to live with us, I was jealous of him because he lived with Mommy and all our other siblings.

I especially wanted to hang out with my oldest brother, Grinnell, because he would buy us ice cream. My favorite memory with Grinnell was at Christmas time. He would take Abe and me to Montego Bay to view the city's Christmas tree. It was one of the highlights of my year because I never really got to experience much because of my grandmother's rules. I would see more of Grinnell when Mommy left for America. I think maybe he wanted Abe to feel safe, but I reaped the benefits as well, because he visited often and brought us gifts. Abe and I loved him. I would see more of my older brother when Mommy left for America.

One evening, Abe and I were walking back from choir practice, when we saw a few of our family members driving from the direction of grandma's house. One of the vehicles stopped; my uncle was in the van, and he told us to get home safely. I knew something was wrong. When we got home, my grandmother looked to be in a somber mood. She told us to get ready for bed. The next morning, my grandmother would tell us that my older brother had been stabbed to death.

According to grandma, after Grinnell was stabbed, a man put him in a shopping cart and pushed him to the hospital while blood was gushing from his ears. When they arrived at the hospital, doctors pronounced him dead. There was nothing the doctors could do because he had already lost a large amount of blood. Abe started crying. I was silent, still processing the information. It was then that my mother decided that she needed all of her children in America with her.

I remember the week leading up to my departure. I could not tell anyone at school that I was going to America. So, I kept mum and told no one.

'Why mi can't tell mi teachas and friends?'
'Because people will try fi kill yuh like dey kill yuh bradda'.

That was the only response I needed for me to keep my mouth shut. I did not want to end up like my brother, so I told no one.

As it got closer to the flight date, it became real that I would soon be in America. I had a vision of what America would be like. There was snow, big buildings, lots of cars, and fast-food places. I would fantasize about our house and the food we would eat. I also thought about living with my mother for the first time, because I had never had that opportunity in Jamaica. Whenever I spoke to her over the phone, she seemed vibrant. She seemed as if she was the complete opposite of my grandmother, who was very strict and religious. I wanted some freedom, or so I thought.

The day before my flight, my aunt and grandma took me and Abe to the beach, because they wanted to celebrate the last time they would see us.

'But, auntie, a nuh di last time yuh a go see wi' I said.
'It is, Wingin, it is. Yuh see yuh madda since she left? she said
'No, but why not?'
'Mi nuh know'.

I didn't quite understand what my aunt meant at the time, but I knew she wanted to enjoy that day with us, so I gave up on questioning her. After we left the beach, we went to eat at Burger King; it was the best burger I had ever had. Later that day, I went to get my hair done before the big day. My hair was dark-brown, natural, and long. It was rare that I could get my hair flat ironed because we did not have the money for that, but my mother wanted to make sure we looked the part. Americans had their hair flat ironed.

On the day of the flight, we met up with a family friend. She was heavy set, her lips were dark without lipstick, and she wore very nice clothes. She looked American. She had tattoos and piercings everywhere on her body. She would be traveling with us and would be the person taking care of us on the flight. She handed my brother and me chewing gum, because she said our ears might pop while we were on the flight, so we should try to chew before taking off.

Grandma went to the airport with us. I was so nervous and scared because I had never been on a plane before. I know Abe was nervous too, but he did not show it; he was smiling and looked at ease. I gave my grandmother a big hug and could see the tears well up in her eyes. She was going to miss me, and I was going to miss her. She was all I knew for the last 11 years, and I was leaving her behind.

The plane was very extravagant. The flight attendants were dressed in purple and black. They had very strong Jamaican accents, so I relaxed once I sat down in my seat. While on the flight, the family friend told us that we would be stopping in Atlanta, Georgia.

I spent the entire plane ride looking out the window.

Once we landed in Atlanta, we went through immigration customs and then transferred to our flight to California. The second flight was less stressful. My brother and I chatted about our first escalator experience and what we would do when we saw our mom. For years, I had dreamt that I would one day live with my mother. There were butterflies in my stomach. A few hours later, we landed at LAX in Los Angeles. We would see Mommy; Scarlet, my younger sister, who was born in America; Kelly; and Kelly's daughter, Brittany, who was also born in America.

Greeting my mother at LAX was the first time I had seen her in years. She did not look like the woman I remembered. She had a large cut in her face, she was very short, and she wore two big bamboo earrings. My mother hugged Abe and squeezed him for a few seconds. I was waiting on my turn to hug her, but it never came. She looked at me and said, 'Hi, Wingin'. Maybe it did not seem appropriate to her. It made me sad, and it became a memory that stayed with me for years.[1]

On our way home from the airport, I stared out the window at the many cars I was seeing. I wondered why I hadn't initiated a hug with my mother, all while taking in the real America. There were so many stop lights, stop signs, rental car places, and fast-food restaurants. I was in awe that the steering wheel was on the left side of the car.

After driving for a few minutes, we pulled up to Van Ness Ave in Inglewood, California. What at first looked like a house, I soon learned, was an apartment. It was the first time I had ever seen numbers on a building. My grandmother's house did not have any numbers on it, and none of the houses in Johns Hall did either' I was intrigued.

'Mommy, dis a yuh house?' I asked
   'No, dis a mi apartment'.
   'Apartment? Wha dat?'
   'Like a house, but it smalla and ada people live yah'.
   'Ada people live in a di house wid us?'
   'No, dey live inna di building'.
   'Wha bout di numba, wah mek it deh yah?'
   'Dat a wi apartment numba. Yuh see di otha ones have numbas too?'
   'Yeah, but why?'
   'So, people cah find it and send witings'.
   'Suh how you send wi tings a Jamaica, because wi house nuh have numbas'.
   'It go a di mailbox. Everybody mail in a Jamaica go a di post office and dey pick it up'.

Once we got inside the apartment, I was in heaven. The walls were painted white, and each room had its own personality. The living room had a brown carpet, Bob Marley pictures on the walls, and a black leather couch. The couch seemed to be something you would see in a magazine, but the thing that caught my eye was the television. It was about 50 inches wide and had a huge back. In Jamaica, my grandmother had a TV that could fit on a nightstand, and we did not get very many channels. I was very sure that this TV had more than a few channels. There was a huge cabinet that was filled with DVDs and cassettes. It gave the living room a very vibrant feeling. The living room also had a glass dining table with four chairs and placemats in front of each chair. The space felt overcrowded, but I was impressed.

I marveled at the kitchen, with its white refrigerator, dishwasher, sink, and multiple cabinets. In the kitchen was a sliding glass door that connected to the outside porch. The flooring on the porch was green.

After leaving the porch, I made my way to see the bedrooms. One bedroom had a huge bed, a dresser, and a closet. This was my mother's room, and her personality shined through because there were jewelry and wigs everywhere. This was the room she shared with my younger sister.

The other room had two beds, a twin-sized and a queen-sized, this would be the room that my younger brother and I would be in. There was a white dresser pushed into the corner. It had pictures on it. The bathroom was right across from the second bedroom. It was on the inside of the apartment, a luxury I was not used to in Jamaica. This bathroom did not need a bucket of water for flushing. All I had to do was put my hand on the handle, and it would do the trick. It was the nicest bathroom I had ever seen in my life. I flushed it three times before my mother came in and said, 'Don't waste di water'.

After a few days in Inglewood, my mother enrolled me in Monroe Magnet Middle School, which was a 35-minute walk from the apartment. The students wore white polo shirts and blue khaki pants for uniforms. We could wear any shoes we wanted. Abe was enrolled at a school a few minutes away from my school. Before signing us up for school, my mom had warned us that she would not be taking us to school every morning, but she would pick us up after school.

The first morning, we were excited to be going to school with our new backpacks and sneakers. Our walk from the apartment to school was a straight shot. It seemed much less traveled than the route we took in Jamaica. We were sure to stop at every stop sign and look both ways before crossing the street. This was something that was ingrained in us as children in Jamaica, because we began walking to school as early as three years old.

I was enrolled in sixth grade. I had already completed the sixth grade in Jamaica, so I was not very happy about repeating it. I had hoped that when I got to America, I would be placed in the seventh grade, but I was wrong. I was disappointed that they did not have a test I could take or another way that I could prove that I belonged in a higher grade. They based their decision on my age and the month of my birthday, which was October. I was not off to a good start.

When I first got to Monroe, I was overwhelmed because of the classes, the teachers, the students, and the accents. I could barely keep up with what the teachers were saying because they spoke so fast. I also never knew where to sit; everyone else sat in groups, I ate lunch by myself for about two weeks. The first day was challenging because I did not know what food to eat. They did not have any Jamaican food at the cafeteria; they had burgers and pizza. While I was excited that I could eat American food, I was used to eating Jamaican patties and coco bread for lunch or fried chicken and rice peas.

The classwork and homework were the easiest work I had ever done in school; I was bored. One day, my English teacher suggested that I enroll in the magnet classes. I had no idea what magnet courses were, but I was happy that the work might be more difficult. The assistant principal told me that I needed to get a permission slip signed before they could enroll me in those classes. So that afternoon, when my mother picked us up from school, I told her my good news. She had no idea what magnet classes were, so I told her she did not need to worry. All she had to do was sign the paper. She signed, and the next day, my class schedule changed.

I enjoyed my new classes; even though the content was still not challenging for me, the students in those classes were very interested in learning. I met Anise, Ebony, Clarissa, Jasmine, Julie, Sheneka, and Raneisha, who became my new friends. All of them were in my classes, and they were very smart. It seemed that I had finally met my tribe and did not have to eat lunch by myself anymore. They loved my accent and would frequently ask me to 'say something in Jamaican'. I would say the same phrase every time, *Wah a gwaan?* It made them laugh every time. We obsessed over our grades in classes and had great relationships with our teachers. We did everything together, and I would learn certain cues from them. They would say, *Let me go home with a C, my mama will whoop my ass,* or *I cannot get suspended because my mama will beat the black off me.* I was getting all As in my classes, and my mother never worried about my report cards. I was not bothered.

During my time at Monroe, I also started playing basketball. My mom bought my brother and me a basketball hoop, and we would play in the back alley by our apartment. I had never heard of basketball before I got to America because we played netball and cricket in Jamaica. But basketball reminded me of netball – it involved the same movements – so I started playing with friends from the neighborhood. Soon, I was one of the best players in the alley. Every evening, I would invite all of our neighbors to come out and play with us. My mom did not like that I was running around 'like a boy', but I kept doing my chores in the house and would go outside to play basketball until the street lights came on. That was enough for her.

During my seventh-grade year, my science teacher and coach of the girls' and boys' basketball teams at Monroe posted flyers around school to announce basketball tryouts. It never crossed my mind that I should try out for the girls' team, but my brother was planning on trying out for the boys' team, so I had to stay after school with him. While he was trying out, I began shooting around and playing by myself. The coach saw me playing and demanded that I join the girls' team. It did not take much convincing. When my brother saw me, he was shocked, but he also knew he would not be embarrassed because his sister could play some ball. The next day, my name was one of the names that made the list for the girls' basketball team.

During my eighth-grade year of middle school, all of my friends had been talking about which high schools they were going to attend. I hadn't given it much thought, because Morningside High School was my home school, and I figured I would attend that school. My friends kept asking me if I was thinking about CAMS (California Academy for Math and Science) or City Honors. Both schools were top high schools in the state at the time. City Honors High School (CHHS) was a new charter school and had attracted much attention because it only offered Advanced Placement and honors courses. However, I did not know much about how the high school system worked in America. In Jamaica, every student took a placement test in sixth grade, and, depending on their score, they were placed in a high school. The students with very high scores went to the most prestigious schools, and the students who did not score very well went to the underserved schools.

Another aspect of the American school system that was new to me was the Grade Point Average system. In Jamaica, students were ranked on the basis of overall average. All my grades from all my classes would be combined to create a percentage, with 100% being the highest and 1% being the lowest. Based on where a student fell in that range, they would be ranked in their grade. I would rank anywhere between second and third places every single year from primary through secondary school.

At first, I did not like America's system because it was unfamiliar, but I grew to admire it because I was able to focus on my work and not worry about being ranked. In Jamaica, ranking was always a stressor, because it could be a true embarrassment to be ranked in last place in your entire grade. I worked hard to ensure that I was a top-ranking student at all times. Fortunately, I did not have to worry too much about this in America.

Eventually, I became curious and started researching high schools and learned that City Honors had a reputation for accepting students with high-grade point averages. I filled out the application and signed my mother's name. I got in. My mother was proud of me. She drove me to school every day.

Everything was going well, until sophomore year when the college conversations became a daily ritual. My counselor and I were having exchanges about my college options. She was very adamant that I would get into college because of my grades and my involvement in sports. I became obsessed with the idea that I could go to college and have a life similar to the Huxtables, the fictional upper middle class Black family on *The Cosby Show*.

As I researched colleges, I learned that most students completed the Free Application for Federal Student Aid (FAFSA) in order to get money to help them pay for college. And to apply for FAFSA, one had to have a social security number. I was curious about what that meant so I asked my mother for my social security number. She told me, very casually, that I did not have one. It felt very harmless.

But I could not shake the feeling, so I went back to her.

'Wingin, yuh no have no social security numba', my mother said with a very irritated look on her face.

'But why not?' I said, very intrigued.

'Because yuh a nuh merican'.

'So, how mi get one? Because mi need one fi go a college'.

'Yuh can't get one'.

I later learned that my mother's casual reveal was more serious than I thought. I was undocumented.

I had just finished my sophomore year at City Honors and could not risk any of my classmates or teachers finding out that I was undocumented. I became ashamed and afraid of my undocumented status. I did not want anyone to know. I thought the best decision was to transfer to a big public school where I could get lost in a sea of students. No one would notice me; I would become invisible. I could hide in the shadows.

That year, I transferred to Leuzinger High School in Hawthorne, California. It was easy to convince my mother to let me transfer schools because we were already moving to Hawthorne to a bigger house, and Leuzinger was just a few minutes away.

When I first enrolled at Leuzinger, I learned that my graduating class had more than 700 students. My plan of becoming invisible was off to a good start. I figured I could enroll in 'normal' classes at my new school, because no one would know that I was a top student at my other school. During my first week at Leuzinger, I had to meet with my new counselor to discuss my class schedule. At CHHS, all of the students were enrolled in the same classes, and there was no distinction about classes. But, at Leuzinger, there were many variations. Some students were enrolled in all Advanced Placement (AP) courses, while others were enrolled in Honors courses and some were even enrolled in a mix of classes. I was not quite sure which category I would fall into, but I knew that, with my transcript, I would be encouraged to take certain courses. I was prepared to argue against that option.

The first time I met with my counselor, Mr. Tovar, he struck me as someone who would be hard to convince that I should enroll in less rigorous courses. He was about six feet tall, Latino, and had a very strong build. Mr. Tovar spoke highly of my grades and was very firm that I was college bound. As he talked, I looked everywhere but at his face. His desk was filled with pictures of his family and scattered letters from past students. His college diploma is framed on his wall. I was not paying attention to him.

'Felecia, are you listening to me?' he would eventually say.
'Yes, sir, I am listening'.
'So, what do you think about this schedule?'

He had designed a schedule with all AP and Honor courses for me. I told him I did not want to be in those classes, and he advised me against that decision. He asked me to give the classes a try. I think he thought I believed they might be difficult, but, in reality, I saw them as pointless if I could not go to college. But I did not want to get into an argument with my counselor, so I accepted the schedule. After I left Mr. Tovar's office that day, I remember feeling sorry for myself, because I did not have anyone to talk to about my situation.

I thought, *Why do all these people have such high hopes for me? If only they knew I was undocumented, they would not care.* I wished everyone would stop telling me what was best for me.

My junior year was nothing like my two previous years in high school. By the end of my first semester, I had failed my two Math courses. It was the first time I had failed a class. I didn't even know how to accept it. It was a strange feeling, like the moment you put on a pair of shoes, which are your size, but instead of fitting like they normally do, they feel tight. The stress of believing that my life was over and that my only options were to return to Jamaica or end up in jail weighed heavily on me, and I could not perform the way I wanted to. I stopped doing my homework and paying attention in class. My grades were unfamiliar to me. I also knew that my next meeting with Mr. Tovar would not go well.

Mr. Tovar was patient but baffled. I could see it in his face. It was clear that he was very disappointed in the way that I had performed that semester. But I was uninterested in talking about my grades, because I still felt sorry for myself. Not to mention that my mother and her then boyfriend were constantly fighting. It was a stressful time at home, and I had no energy to be brave. I only had the energy to exist.

During one of our scheduled meetings during my second semester, Mr. Tovar began asking me questions about my college list. I had not thought about my college list because I had taken away the option from myself. So, as Mr. Tovar's mouth moved, I practiced how I would tell him about my undocumented status and my mother's relationship with her abusive boyfriend. But, as I replayed what the conversation would sound like, the worst scenarios played out in my head.

What if I told Mr. Tovar the truth and he reported my family? What if he got us deported? What if he no longer recognized my potential? What if he no longer thought that I was deserving of college?
    'You are better than these grades that you received this semester and I know it, because you came here with all As', Mr. Tovar said.

He went on and on about the colleges that would be best for me.
    I remember getting up and closing Mr. Tovar's door and then sitting back down.

'I am undocumented. I am from Jamaica. I can't go to college. I would love to, but I can't', I said.

I felt like a criminal disclosing my status to him. However, a weight was lifted from me. Mr. Tovar leaned forward. His eyes were focused on mine, and I could feel his spirit piercing through my soul.

'Felecia, thank you for sharing your story with me'.

Mr. Tovar proceeded to tell me that I could still make college a reality, but he was very honest about the lack of access to aid, which would make my transition to college difficult but not impossible. He also thought it was wise that I joined the only support group on campus for undocumented students. They referred to themselves as the DREAMers club. Before I got to ask more about the DREAMers club, Mr. Tovar reassured me that everything would be fine. He told me stories about his childhood and encouraged me to continue believing that my life was bigger than my circumstances. He repeated that I could still go to college, and while there were many barriers because I was not eligible for federal financial aid, I would make it. He did not make it sound easy, but he made it sound possible. All I needed was an assurance that it was possible.
    After he told his stories, he continued talking about the DREAMers club on campus and how beneficial he believed it would be for me. I was excited to join because I did not know that there were other undocumented

students at my school. That day, when I left Mr. Tovar's office, I felt a new sense of hope. There were other students like me.

The next day, Mr. Tovar introduced me to the advisor for the DREAMers club. The advisor made me feel welcome and informed me that the other students would be happy for me to join. On my first day in the group, I realized that not only was I the only Jamaican, I was also the only Black person. My minority status felt further pronounced, as not one person in that group looked like me. I did not want to disappoint Mr. Tovar by quitting the group, but I felt so out of place. I hated going to those meetings. It was as if I was a different kind of undocumented, and I did not fit in. Even though I felt like an outcast, the advisor was always very helpful; he constantly met with me one on one, especially after I stopped going to the meetings.

During the second semester of my junior year of high school, I worked very hard in my Math class. I stayed after school and met with my teachers because I wanted to get back on track. I had a new found hope of going to college, and while things at home were still problematic, I held on to the stability of school and the fact that I could control the grades I received. My teachers were impressed, and I finished the semester with all As. Mr. Tovar was very happy.

By my senior year, I had a new friend, Winston. He and I had met in AP History that year. His family was from Barbados. He was drawn to me because I was from Jamaica, and I was drawn to him because he was cute and kind. Winston had a strong accent, a neat fade, a beautiful smile, and was very confident in his walk. Winston and I did everything together. We were inseparable. Everyone thought we were dating. We tried dating each other for about five days, and it was a disaster, so we became best friends. Winston was my community at Leuzinger.

By this time, Mr. Tovar and I were working diligently to narrow down my college list and draft my personal statement. We were having a hard time with my personal statement because I was unwilling to divulge information about my immigrant status. Mr. Tovar challenged me to include my entire story because he claimed it spoke volumes about how I was able to perform so well in school while balancing my home life. I disagreed with him. I did not want to spotlight my undocumented status. Every time I would write a draft of my personal statement, Mr. Tovar would kindly suggest that I go deeper with my story. He wanted the admission counselors to know me from the words on the paper. I would not give in.

Without documentation, I found myself in a precarious position as a high school senior, applying to colleges without access to the state and federal financial resources that were available to my classmates. I applied for many private scholarships. However, the scholarships intended for undocumented students were often closed to me because I was a Black immigrant from

Jamaica; the scholarship applications stipulated that applicants must be of Hispanic origin. Even so, I applied for hundreds of other scholarships. I spent many sleepless nights as a high school senior.

During my final semester of high school, the college decisions poured in. My first acceptance letter was from University of California, Riverside. I remember coming home from school, opening the big envelope, and reading the words, 'We are pleased to confirm your admittance to the University of California, Riverside'.[2] I screamed and jumped for joy. Then, I ran to my mother's room to show her the letter. She was happy for me but did not quite understand what it meant. The next day, I brought the letter to Mr. Tovar, knowing he would be proud. We celebrated and then reality set in. They did not offer me any scholarships.

After the UCR acceptance, I was denied from all other UC schools. Mr. Tovar and I were shocked. He suggested an appeal to UCLA, the school he wanted me to attend. He did not understand why I did not get accepted to any of my top schools. I had a 4.6 GPA, played sports, had a strong story, and I knew I could add value to any campus. It was disappointing, but a part of me felt like I did not get in because I was undocumented, scored poorly on my SAT, and did not have the finances to prove that I could pay for school. Still, Mr. Tovar was immovable that we appealed UCLA's decision. We did. The decision remained the same.

Soon after my rejection from the UC's, I received an acceptance from Whittier College. Whittier is a small liberal arts college in Whittier, CA, about 30 minutes south of Los Angeles. Whittier offered me a sizable scholarship, but I could not afford a private school. Then, I received an acceptance from California Lutheran University, another private institution. They also offered me a considerable scholarship, a financial package bigger than Whittier. I was not excited about Cal Lutheran; I only applied because they sent me a fee waiver so I could submit a free application. I knew nothing about the institution. I felt defeated. But, Cal Lutheran was Mr. Tovar's only hope for me to go to a four-year institution. He felt he had failed me. He did not understand why the institutions I applied for did not give me better financial aid. I found it to be a blessing that he cared that much.

Within a day of Cal Lutheran's acceptance, Mr. Tovar introduced me to another college counselor at Leuzinger. Mr. Tovar wanted me to meet this counselor because she knew a family who graduated from Cal Lutheran and thought it would be a good idea for me to meet them. I did not see any harm in her suggestion.

When I met with Ms. Green, she told me that she had spoken to Shawn Howie, the man who was her neighbor in Santa Monica. He was a proud alumna of Cal Lutheran. His wife and four children also graduated from Cal Lutheran. She also told me he graduated from Harvard University with an

MBA, but no one would know because he only talked about Cal Lutheran. Ms. Green believed Mr. Howie could help me get additional aid, which would make my transition to Cal Lutheran more doable. I thought her idea was far-fetched, but I was hopeful. She gave me his number and told me to give him a call.

That night, I called Mr. Howie, and it went to voicemail. I left a message. I don't remember the context of what I said. The next day, Mr. Howie called me back and was impressed that I even made the call. He told me that if I could find a way to visit Cal Lutheran, he would give me a tour of the university. I told him I would find a way.

At that time, I was living with Pastor Chaney and his family during the week because my mother had moved to Lake Elsinore, which was almost two hours away from Leuzinger, and I needed to finish my senior year at the same school.[3] I had met Pastor Chaney during my junior year at Leuzinger. He was my English teacher, and he was also a pastor of a local church in Los Angeles. He invited me to church often, and I always turned down the request. However, one Sunday, I made the decision to go because I was feeling sorry for myself, and faith was always there in the background. I fell in love with the idea of community and depending on a God that was bigger than me. Pastor Chaney became a father figure. So, during my senior year when I needed a place to stay so that I could have an easier commute to school, he and his wife opened up his home to me. I stayed with them during the week, sleeping on a couch in the den, and went to my mother's on Friday nights. My mother did not like what I was doing because she wanted me to be home, but at this point, she knew I was determined to go to college, and I would make decisions that would allow that dream to become a reality.

That day after I got off the call with Mr. Howie, I called Pastor Chaney to tell him the good news. He and his family drove me to Cal Lutheran to meet with Shawn Howie and their family the next week. I remember my first-time meeting Shawn. He was white, about 5′5″, and he had a dog with him. I was terrified of dogs because I was chased by one in Jamaica. Shawn was respectful of my fear and kept the dog on a leash.

Cal Lutheran's campus was beautiful, filled with trees, paved sidewalks, big buildings, and a peaceful vibe. Shawn gave me a private tour of the campus while I shared my story with him. I held nothing back. He was very intrigued. I shook his hand, and he told me that he would be in touch. On our drive back to LA that day, Shawn called and told me that he and his family would like to help make Cal Lutheran a reality for me. I could live with them, and he would pay whatever was left of my tuition and fees. I cried. He said it would be like a loan.[4] I was going to college. On May 1, 2010, I committed to California Lutheran University without knowing much else. I would be the first in my family to go to college.

Within a month after committing to Cal Lutheran, I graduated from Leuzinger High school with a 4.6 GPA, ranked #4 in my class of over 700 students. My family was in the audience for my graduation: my mother, Kelly, Brittany, Scarlet, and Abe. They were proud. Mr. Tovar was delighted for me. Ms. Green was hopeful for me. I was scared, but I would still trudge on.

Notes

The stories that are told in this chapter are from my perspective and could be interpreted differently by others. To protect the identity of my family and friends, some are disguised with pseudonyms.

1. Over the last few years, we hug frequently.
2. Quote here is an approximation.
3. I would go to my mom's on the weekends.
4. He never asked me to pay back the loan. It was a gift of service.

2

COLLEGE REALIZED AND THE BARRIERS TO PERSISTENCE

I started my college journey at California Lutheran University in the summer of 2010.[1] I remember walking around campus in my big gold bamboo earrings, my gold chain with a *Felecia* pendant, and my pink snapback hat. There was a bounce in my step; one of my dreams was happening in real time, and I felt invincible. There was no more hope of college; I was here.

Before the fall semester began, I met Mark Warren, who was then the Associate Vice President of Enrollment at Cal Lutheran. Shawn introduced me to Mark just a few weeks after I toured the campus with him. Shawn thought Mark would be a good person for me to know because I needed as many people in my corner as possible if I was going to successfully persist at Cal Lutheran. He was right. As Anthony Jack, former Harvard Professor and author of the *Privileged Poor* noted in his book, when some students first step foot on a college campus, it looks, feels, and functions like nothing they have experienced before; he refers to those students as the doubly disadvantaged, those who are both poor and unfamiliar with this new world (pg. ii). Cal Lutheran's campus was like nothing I had experienced before. Thousand Oaks, where almost every face I saw was white, was in stark contrast to my neighborhood in Inglewood where almost everyone was Black or Brown. Besides Shawn and his family, I had never spent significant time with any other white person. By Jack's definition, I was doubly disadvantaged. However, having Mark in my corner was a privilege.

Mark organized for me to start a summer course, *Introduction to Christianity*, so I could get acclimated to the college culture, adjust to the coursework, and familiarize myself with a campus that would be dominated by white faces. Before the fall semester began, I knew where to find the

DOI: 10.4324/9781003442998-3

cafeteria, the library, the gym, and the dormitories, giving me a head start that would be beneficial for my collegiate path.

Beyond the logistical head start, I would also form an important relationship with Dr. Sebastian Taylor, my *Introduction to Christianity* professor. Dr. Taylor was white, nerdy-looking yet handsome. He had a quiet confidence about him. Our first assignment was for us to write to him. He wanted us to tell him who we were – our background, our experiences, our challenges – and tell him what we knew about the subject and our thoughts on it. I thought it was an odd assignment for a college class, but it turned out to be the most formative assignment for my learning. Dr. Taylor used my experience to align my learning. He did not lower the bar; he met me where I was, and I needed it. My writing was not strong, but Dr. Taylor's guidance provided me with the tools I needed to seek support from the writing center without feeling embarrassed. He told me that college writing was different from high school, and it was important to ask for help. I would be working twice as hard as my peers to keep up, and I should lean on the resources available. Dr. Taylor collaborated with me and challenged me. His support during that summer class would influence how I sought help moving forward, a tool that not many low-income, Black, undocumented immigrant students know to use while in college.

Although I had learned important academic tools over the summer, I struggled to keep up with my classes during my first year at Cal Lutheran. I stayed in the library for hours at a time. I was determined not to fail, but the classes were difficult. One class in particular, *World Civilization*, was the hardest class I took at Cal Lutheran; on the first assignment, I received a 2/5. The professor said it was poorly written and lacked imagination. I began going to the writing center to get the support on all of my assignments before submitting them. On my next assignment, I received a 3/5. Soon, I got a 4, and, eventually, I received a 5 – but never consistently. This was a new reality I would have to get used to at Cal Lutheran; I was not accustomed to the rigor of work that was expected of me.

Although my courses were challenging and took most of my time, I knew that it was important to find time to join student groups on campus. I joined the Black Student Union (BSU); I needed a sense of community and belonging, and BSU seemed like it could provide that. On a campus where I was often the only Black student in all of my classes or in any casual space, BSU allowed me to interact with other Black students and attend events and outings that contributed to my sense of belonging on campus. One in particular was an outing in the mosh pit at the Black Entertainment Television (BET) awards, where I shouted at Beyonce during a commercial break to express my love for her.[2] In addition to attending events, we discussed our experiences as Black students in a predominately white institution;[3] for instance, professors would sometimes call on us to answer questions when the conversation was centered around Blackness, as if we spoke for all Black people. There were always conversations about issues that affected us on campus and issues that affected the greater Black community. However, we never discussed immigration even though there were Black immigrants in the group. The group activities were centered around the Black American experience, and while I still felt a sense of deep connection to Black American culture, I longed for activities to be centered around the Black Caribbean experience or the Black immigrant experience – experiences that were uniquely different from those of my peers. After all, I grew up in America and understood what it meant to be Black in America. Yet, I was also Jamaican and an immigrant; however, when others saw me, they simply saw me as Black. I yearned to be recognized as someone with intersecting identities, but it never happened.

I also joined the DREAMers club for undocumented students. The meetings were held in the chapel, and not many students knew it existed. Every student who joined the DREAMers club also had access to the food pantry in the chapel that was specifically for undocumented students. We did not have any public events, out of fear of being identified as undocumented. The events were private and intimate, and I did not enjoy them because none of the activities accounted for my Blackness. Reminiscent of my high school experience, I was the only Black student in the student organization. I felt out of place, like an outsider. I did not belong. My peers would often speak Spanish, and I would feel an instant sense of isolation. In that group, we never discussed the diversity of the immigrant journey; the discussions were focused on those who migrated from Hispanic countries. I felt lost.

In BSU, I felt connected but not recognized; in the DREAMers organization, I felt ignored and invisible. I longed for community and belonging, but it was nowhere. Both experiences contributed to a difficult first year at Cal Lutheran.

Overall, my first year was more challenging than I had expected. I felt isolated and alone. I did not have many friends, and the ones I did have did not know about my status. I was no longer the smartest student in any room; everyone was steps ahead of me. In hopes of not falling short, my life was consumed with my academic work; I made no time for fun. After all, I could not fail my mother, family, the Howies, the Chaneys, and the other administrators at Cal Lutheran who were supporting me. I had hoped college would be magical, but it just felt overwhelming.

One day, after a tough day on campus, I went to see Mark Warren for one of our regularly scheduled meetings. He was invested in my success, and he wanted to make sure Cal Lutheran would get a good return on their investment. I showed up to his office, defeated and confused. *Why did*

I think I could make it in college? My mother had not graduated high school. My father never made it to high school. My older brother was stabbed to death, and my other siblings hadn't attempted college.[4] *I was in over my head to think I could.* I sensed Mark could see the stress in my eyes because he closed his office door and asked for an update on my experience so far. I broke down and started crying. I was overwhelmed with emotions. He proceeded to ask what I was doing for fun, a question I thought was ill fitted for the moment. I told him I did not have much time for fun. Mark gently told me that the only way I would make it at CLU was to own the fact that it was hard and to find an activity that would take me away from my studies. I thought basketball was the sure answer; I had played it in high school and really enjoyed it. He told me to learn something new and suggested we play tennis. I had never played tennis; the only thing I knew about the sport was that Venus and Serena Williams dominated.

That same evening, Mark took me to the tennis court at Cal Lutheran, and he taught me what he knew about tennis. We probably spent an hour playing that day, and for that one hour, I did not think about the weight of the world. I wanted that feeling again. So for the remainder of the semester, I would go to the tennis courts on my own, whenever I felt defeated. Playing tennis became my favorite way to relax; I even enrolled in tennis for a class during my second semester. Tennis saved me. To this day, I keep two tennis rackets in the trunk of my car.

The next two years contained their own joys and challenges, but one challenge loomed: my undocumented status.

Being undocumented was a thorn in my side. While all my friends had cars and would commute freely, I had no driver's license and always had to depend on someone. I had no freedom. In order for me to get groceries, I would have to make appointments with Susan, Shawn Howie's wife, for her to take me to the grocery store. For me to visit the Chaney's, I had to ask them to pick me up from Cal Lutheran, which was a long drive in heavy traffic on the 405 freeway. In order to see my family, I had to ask my brother Abe to pick me up from campus, which was a two-hour drive for him. I felt like a burden, and I hated it.

My undocumented status was my biggest secret and shame. It was the part of my identity that I could not come to peace with. It limited my opportunities – not just academically but socially as well. I could not do things my friends were doing, and I could not tell them why. '*Come see this R-rated movie with us*', my friends would say, but I couldn't go because I did not have identification to show. But because I hadn't told my friends about my status, I would always respond, 'I don't want to see that movie'. '*Come to the club with us tonight*', they would say. I would always say, 'I don't feel like it'. Even though I wanted to go to a lounge or a bar with my friends, I could not risk it. It felt debilitating to say no to all the fun experiences my friends were having, but I knew the stakes were higher for me. I wasn't just Black, I was undocumented; being caught with a fake ID would be worse for me than it would be for my friends.

Being undocumented also prevented me from working on campus. Professors and other advisors would ask me, 'Why don't you have a job on campus?' But my response would always be, 'I need to focus on my studies'.

It was a terrible feeling to continuously lie, but I did not know how anyone would respond if I shared my biggest secret, until one day, I did.

Dr. Moren was a Cuban, about 5'8", slim, and very smart. I was enrolled in his *Introduction to Sociology* course during my second summer session.[5] He was very attentive to the students in his course, and he was especially attuned to what I needed as a student. I was the only Black student in his class. Dr. Moren and I would have extensive conversations after class, and he was determined that I should major in Political Science and intern with his department. Whenever he mentioned working with the department, I would deflect. One day, in class, we were discussing undocumented students, and he was very clear on his stance about undocumented students. His vocal support for the group made me feel a sense of safety, so I disclosed to him that I was undocumented. Dr. Moren was supportive and thanked me for sharing. He became my advisor and one of my biggest advocates at Cal Lutheran. Dr. Moren also helped me gain my first internship on campus, with the Center for Equality and Justice. The internship was unpaid because of my legal status, but we both thought it would be good for future opportunities. The internship brought me a sense of belonging, and I would brag to my friends about it. There was a sense of normalcy.

Over the next two years at Cal Lutheran, I performed fairly well in my classes, continued participating in BSU, distanced myself from the DREAMers club, interned with the Center for Equality and Justice, continued playing tennis, enrolled in additional summer courses, and rarely partied (not something I am proud of).

My third and final year at Cal Lutheran quickly approached. During that year, immigrant youth fought for Deferred Action for Childhood Arrivals (DACA) and moved former President Barack Obama to use his executive power to give young immigrants who were brought to this country (as children) an opportunity to be free from deportation and to work in this country we call our home. However, many political pundits had doubts about DACA and warned people like myself not to apply. The news stories about the policy declared, '*President Obama only passed DACA for reelection purposes*'; '*If these young people apply for DACA, they are putting themselves at risk of deportation, the government will have their information*'; '*Undocumented youth should wait for a more permanent policy*'; '*A republican administration can rescind DACA'*. The headlines terrified me, but not more than wanting some freedom to exist as my peers did.

In the summer of 2012, I reluctantly applied for DACA. I was tired of living in the shadows. In order to apply, I had to go back to Monroe Middle School to get school records to prove that I had been a student there since 2003. The Howies paid $295[6] for me to get a background check. The entire process took about six months. I still remember the day I got my approval letter. I had just gotten home from summer school, and Susan had left the letter on the dining room table for me. I looked at the letter for several minutes before I opened it.

I was approved. '*In the case of Felecia S. Russell, we have decided to defer your case for two years. This approval does not guarantee citizenship*'.[7] I screamed. Susan ran to the kitchen.

'I was approved', I said while jumping and screaming.
'I am so happy for you! We need to celebrate!' said Susan.
'Yes, I would love that', I said as tears were falling from my eyes.

Susan gave me a hug, and I proceeded to text Uncle Shawn; by this time, he was no longer Mr. Howie, but Uncle Shawn. I also texted Pastor Chaney and my mother the good news.

DACA opened up so many doors for me. In November 2012, I took the California driving test and passed it on my first attempt. That same year, I applied for a job on campus with the Forest Fitness Center. Soon, I was working the 5 am shift with the football and basketball athletes. All of my paychecks went to law school applications and graduation necessities.

However, while I had received temporary status through DACA, my older sister, Kelly, was about to be deported back to Jamaica. On August 8, 2012, Kelly was arrested by ICE. It was the same evening I was listening to a webinar about the new DACA policy. My cell phone was in my bedroom upstairs, and I was downstairs with my computer listening to the webinar. Abe was sitting a few feet away on the couch, watching the Olympics. Abe received a call from Mommy; she was crying as she said, 'Kelly is in jail. She is in immigration'. I felt my heart drop, and I became weak. All I could think about was the fact that I would not be able to help my sister. I had not graduated yet, and while I had plans to become an immigration lawyer after much convincing from Uncle Shawn, I was far away from that goal.

Kelly was held in immigration jail for over eight months before she was deported back to Jamaica. While she was in jail, I would frequently talk to Kelly on the phone. I knew she was lonely, but she remained in good spirits. When Kelly was released, she was placed on a ten-year ban from

America. She has been living in Jamaica since, a tough reality for Mommy, who wanted a different life for all of her children.

Prior to Kelly's arrest, Oakley, my older brother, had spent a year in an immigration detention facility as well before he was deported back to Jamaica, so it was not the first time I had someone go through the process. Both times were devastating and traumatic. However, I was fed up and exhausted that I had to go through this another time. Kelly's experience was especially upsetting because I was very close to finishing my college degree, and it felt like a huge roadblock.

On May 18, 2013, I graduated from California Lutheran University with a 3.86 grade point average, Magna Cum Laude. Because of all the summer courses I had taken and the two college courses I had taken in high school, I graduated in three years with a bachelor's degree in Political Science, Legal Studies, and Law and Public Policy. Although I was proud of this accomplishment, I did not enjoy the day. I kept thinking, *It would be better if I had one more year to save money; I don't have a car; where will I live?; how will I pay for law school?*

Three years prior, when I graduated high school, I was caught in a web of doubt, wondering where my life would take me; on the day of my college graduation, I was again preoccupied by what was next, a step I had yet to figure out. I was proud that I would be the first in my family to graduate from college, but I did not have a job or the money to pay for law school.

Graduation day was also lonely since I was experiencing it without my classmates and friends. I was not graduating with the class that I came in with, so I did not know anyone. I was graduating in three years, a goal Mark Warren and others had set out for me to accomplish, and while well-intentioned, it left me without community and not many friends on graduation day. I felt unsatisfied with the moment.

I don't remember much of the ceremony, but Mommy, Abe, Scarlet, Winston, the Chaneys, and the Howies all made it to my graduation. The Howies had arranged for me to have a graduation party at their house after the ceremony, and I was looking forward to it. Mommy made brown stew chicken, curry goat, oxtails, jerk chicken, rice and peas, cabbage, and festival – some of my favorite Jamaican dishes. Mommy showed love through her food, and this was her way of showing she was proud of me.

There are many times I wish I could go back to that day and experience it all over again because I would bask in my accomplishment and give myself credit for being the first in my family to earn a college degree. As a Black, undocumented woman, I had accomplished something many people would have not thought possible; even I didn't always believe that it was possible. However, I did not seize the moment. Now, when I think of it, I realize the disservice I did to myself. If I could go back, I would tell my 21-year-old self,

> *Felecia, I know you feel alone right now. You feel like you need to have it all figured out, all graduates do. But enjoy this moment. Look into the faces of the people around you. Smile. Take some pictures, even with people you don't know. Invite all your friends from Monroe, City Honors, and Leuzinger. Invite Mr. Tovar and Ms. Green; they would be so proud of you. Do not dim this moment because you don't know what is next. You have come this far and this is not it for you. You are not a part of the dysfunctional cycle of poverty, incarceration, and pain. You have broken that cycle, you can breathe. It will all be okay. Enjoy the party. Jump in the pool. Laugh and thank your community. They don't owe you a car or money for law school. Be grateful. Be in the moment.*

I think 21-year-old Felecia would have loved to hear those words.

Notes

The stories that are told in this chapter are from my perspective and could be interpreted differently by others. To protect the identity of my family and friends, certain names used in this chapter are pseudonyms, and other identifying descriptors were disguised.

1. California Lutheran University is now an HSI (Hispanic Serving Institution).
2. She looked at me and said she loved me too!
3. California Lutheran University is now an HSI (Hispanic Serving Institution).
4. Years later, Abe and Scarlet would go on to accomplish their college degrees. Scarlet also earned a master's degree in 2023.
5. Mark Warren organized for me to be in summer school again.
6. The price is now $495 for renewals.
7. Quote here is an approximation.

Reference

Jack, A. A. (2020). *The privileged poor: How elite colleges are failing disadvantaged students.* Harvard University Press.

3

THE HOPE OF GRADUATE SCHOOL

Prior to my graduation from Cal Lutheran, I took the LSAT twice. Unfortunately, I failed miserably and could not score above a 153.[1] In my mind, this deemed me not law school material. I still applied to law schools but was rejected by almost all of them. It was a repeat of my senior year of high school. I just was not good enough.

Eventually, I was accepted to Valparaiso University Law School in Valparaiso, Indiana, and Golden Gate University Law School in San Francisco, California. Just as I had failed to get into UCLA or any of the top schools on my list in high school, I had failed to get into any of my top law school choices. But, I decided I had to go with the options I had. Valparaiso seemed like the best fit, but I did not have the money to buy a plane ticket, so I crossed it off the list. That left Golden Gate as my only option. Golden Gate University offered me a small scholarship, but even with DACA, I still did not qualify for federal financial aid or loans so the financial challenge remained.[2] I submitted my $600 deposit to secure my spot while I figured out how I would make my new dream a reality.

After graduation, I felt completely lost being back in the real world. I had moved out of my campus dorm and was back at Mommy's. In a way, living on campus was a reprieve for me; I was away from all the stressors at home; it was where I had the freedom to exist without the weight of the world. I no longer had a place of refuge. While at Mommy's, I applied for scholarships to help fund law school at Golden Gate in the fall; I did not receive any of them. I applied for jobs at El Pollo Loco, KFC, and Target so that I would have money to pay my expenses; I did not get any of the jobs.

DOI: 10.4324/9781003442998-4

Because I had paid my security deposit for Golden Gate, I was receiving their emails about orientation. I wanted to go, but it was in San Francisco, and I needed a plane ticket or a car to attend. Additionally, I needed a place to stay while I was there. In the midst of applying for jobs and trying to find a way to go to San Francisco for orientation, I envisioned a different future. *What would it be like if I decided to pursue my master's?* I was also getting emails from Pepperdine University about their master's degree in Public Policy; I decided to apply so that I would have another option.

As a recent college graduate, I was completely lost, and I would have gone in any direction if it meant I would feel worthy of having a college degree. One of the biggest mistakes I made as an undergraduate student was putting too much emphasis on getting good grades and not spending enough time learning about what I enjoyed, what gave me joy, or envisioning what I could see myself doing in the future. It would have been a privilege, and I did not have the capacity to visualize purpose; I was merely trying to survive.

During those summer days in 2013, I often thought about the tremendous amount of support I received during my time at Cal Lutheran, but I realized that I did not receive information on how to move beyond college. There were no courses on the importance of networking or how to transition from college to the real world. It was as if I had a life vest for the boat ride, but the moment we landed, someone took it away from me. Now, I was swimming in the ocean, struggling to swim without a life vest.

While I felt lost in this transition, one fact remained true: I had people who were invested in my success at every step of the way, and they would come through for me, over and over again.

That summer, my best friend, Winston, bought me a ticket to San Francisco to go to orientation at Golden Gate. While I was at orientation, I knew there was no way I could be a law student without access to a full scholarship or loans and federal financial aid. That weekend, I laid that dream to rest. It was time to pivot.

I got my acceptance letter from Pepperdine University on July 13, 2013. With the acceptance came a substantial scholarship that would make my transition to Pepperdine more manageable than law school. With the scholarship, I would owe $6,000 per year. I expressed to Winston my desire to go to Pepperdine, but I did not have the money to pay the remaining cost. Winston encouraged me to pursue the dream even though it seemed impossible. He drove me to Malibu to visit Pepperdine, a beautiful campus that overlooks the beach.

Two weeks after our visit, Winston was generous enough to help me pay my deposit. He was a huge member of my community, and he would continue to be instrumental in my journey throughout the coming years.

Paying the deposit was a step on faith. I had no idea where the money would come from to afford it or how I would get to campus for class. After all, Pepperdine was in Malibu, nearly 45 minutes away from the Los Angeles area, and I did not have a car. Unlike my start at Cal Lutheran, where I had support and a vision for how I would graduate, Pepperdine was more of an unrealistic shot in the dark. There was no plan in place, so I had to rely on my faith.

Faith has always played a major role in my life. Grandma introduced me to God and the church from an early age. In grandma's home, we started each day with a morning devotion; Mama and I woke up at 5 am to read the Bible, sang songs of worship and praise, and got on our knees to say a prayer to God for his protection and forgiveness. It was a ritual that I embraced, in part, because I loved the connection it gave me to my grandmother and the hope the prayers gave me to imagine a life where we always had what we needed. In addition to our devotions, Mama and I always went to church on Saturdays. I loved the church and even asked to be baptized when I was ten years old, a decision that my grandmother embraced but one that shocked Mommy. I remember telling Mama I wanted to get baptized. She replied,

'Yuh know wha dat mean?'
'Yea, Jesus dead fi mi', I said.
'Mi go tell yuh madda, but yea wi fi do it'.

Mommy did not protest; at the time, she was already living in America. But, she did seem concerned that I was too young to make the decision. Nonetheless, I got baptized a week after that discussion.

While my grandmother's house was strict in our devotion to God, in Mommy's household, we did not perform our faith in the same way. Mommy made it known that she believed in God, but we rarely went to church or did devotions; when I moved in with Mommy as an 11-year-old, I enjoyed that freedom. Whenever I would talk on the phone with my grandma, she would express her disappointment that I was no longer in the church. Her expectation of church for me felt like rules I had to follow to be good with God. I asked Mommy to take me to church a few times, and she did, but it didn't feel as important to honor those rituals anymore; I did not push for them. I thought, *God still loves me even if I am not in church*. From age 11 to 17, I was out of the church, and it was freeing.

However, when I was a senior in high school, I joined Galilee Baptist Church. The Baptist Church had fewer rules than Seventh Day Adventist. As a Seventh Day Adventist, I had to stay in the house on Friday evenings, and I could not engage in social gatherings on Saturdays; Saturday was honored as the Sabbath. However, honoring the Sabbath was not a major point of contention in the Baptist Church.

Joining Galilee was not what my grandmother expected because it was not a Seventh Day Adventist church, but I had grown to only subscribe to what made sense for me, and that my grandma understood. She would say, '*A bettah yuh go a Sunday church than nuh go a church at all*'.

I continued to be a regular member of Galilee even while I was at Cal Lutheran. I attended church once per month, paid tithes and offerings, and went to Bible studies when I visited the Chaneys. The church members at Galilee were all very proud of me and made it their duty to honor my accomplishments in church. They saw me as a product of their prayers and belief in God. I also saw myself as a product of prayers and hard work. I liked going to Galilee; being in church gave me peace that while I was Black and undocumented, God had specifically ordained my steps. This belief mainly came from my favorite verse, Jeremiah 29:11, which states, '*For I know the plans I have for you, declares the Lord, plans to prosper you, give you hope and a future, not to harm you*'. Even when I was discouraged, those words served as inspiration; I held on to them and believed them to be true.

As it got closer to my start date at Pepperdine, I was still unsure of how everything was going to work out. I needed a job so that I would have money to pay my living expenses and the remainder of tuition, a car to commute to Malibu, and a place to live. I had nothing, so I shared it with a church member. This church member was a school teacher, had a loud voice with a vibrant spirit, and was an active member at Galilee. After sharing my struggles with her, I got a call from her the next day, offering to get me a job at McDonalds. This is how 'church' people were. They wanted to help.

I did not want a job at McDonalds, but I was desperate.

She drove me to McDonalds, and I did an interview with the branch manager. The manager offered me the job within three minutes of starting the interview; he told me that he was giving me the job because it seemed like I needed it, but he did not expect me to be at McDonalds for long. I began working at McDonalds three weeks after the interview, a reality I was ashamed of.

Now that I had a job, I needed to find a place to live. The church member drove me around Los Angeles to go apartment hunting. We were trying to find someone who would rent me a room for $300–$450 a month, which was wishful thinking in Los Angeles. Yet, as faith would have it, we found someone who was willing to rent me a room for $500 within a week of searching. The woman's apartment was about 20 minutes from a bus stop that had a route to Malibu. We could not pass up the opportunity. The church member negotiated my monthly rent down to $400 and paid it for the first month.

By the time I started my graduate college journey at Pepperdine, in August 2013, I had a job and a place to stay.

I was taking the bus to and from Malibu every day and walking the rest of the way. It was a long and arduous commute. During my night walks, Pastor Chaney and I would talk on the phone. Those conversations were therapeutic for me because I was having a hard time balancing school and work. There were many lonely nights where I cried on my walks. Some nights, while walking home, helicopters were flying overhead; other times, I would see a news van drive past me as they rushed to a scene. I often felt self-doubt; voices in my head would tell me that I was not good enough and that I would continue a cycle of poverty and dysfunction. It did not matter that I had graduated college; I was consumed by all my fears and doubts.

I carried a lot of fear about my undocumented status. Again, I did not tell my classmates and friends about my status, and I feared them finding out. My undocumented status felt like a burden that made everything harder. It even affected my area of study; I didn't feel that I could focus on international policy because I was unable to travel abroad.[3] As a young graduate student, I made sure to not do anything that could jeopardize my future. Most of the decisions I made were predicated on my fear about my immigrant status. I was scared to major in international policy, so I focused on state and local policy. It felt safe.

But, safety was limiting. Hiding was draining. I did not want to exist in the shadows anymore. I wanted to accept all parts of me, even the parts I did not embrace.

I decided to tell Winston about my immigration status. One evening, I called him and disclosed my immigrant status to him. I immediately felt a sense of relief. In our conversation, his continued support for me did not waver. He saw my undocumented status as a blessing that God was using to propel me to new heights; while I disagreed, I received his words. Winston and I did not have an affectionate relationship; we had a direct one. There was no crying or hugging, just encouragement to keep going.

The conversation with Winston gave me courage to make a tough decision; within a few months of working at McDonalds, I quit. I then applied for three jobs on campus. Within a few weeks, I began working as a shuttle driver for the campus shuttle service, a cashier at the cafeteria and Jamba Juice, and a student worker in the Drescher library. I was easily working over 40 hours per week, which was forbidden by the university; however, I needed the money, so I applied for a waiver for extreme circumstances, and it was approved. Between taking classes and working three jobs, my schedule was extremely demanding and barely sustainable, but I needed the money to pay for school. The money from those jobs helped to cover rent and other living expenses for the first semester of graduate school.

During that first semester, I also continued applying for scholarships. I was interested in the Momentum Millennium Foundation Scholarship, a $6,000 scholarship, but they had a U.S. citizen requirement that I did not meet. However, I really needed more money to continue school, so I submitted an application and noted that I was a DACA recipient, not a citizen. Just four days after I submitted my application, I got an email confirming that I made it to the interview round. I was interviewed by one person who made me feel like I had been chosen for the scholarship before I walked out of the interview. One day after my interview, I got another email confirming that I was chosen as a Brightest Scholar recipient. The $6,000 award covered the remainder of tuition for the first year of my program.

My next task was to secure a car. My schedule depended on the bus schedule, which meant I could not spend my time as I wished. I could not join student organizations because I could miss the bus. I could not spend time in the library, which was a quiet place to study, because I could miss the bus. Not having a car was restrictive. But, after expressing my struggles to a classmate, she told me she was selling her car for $250 because the transmission was unreliable. I purchased the car and received the freedom I had always dreamed of.

With only a few weeks left in my first semester of graduate school, I had a car and was able to register for my second semester as a result of the Momentum scholarship. During the winter break, I set out to find a new place to live to lessen my commute. I also wanted to build community on campus; a sense of belonging was instrumental to my Cal Lutheran experience, and I wanted that at Pepperdine. At the time, Winston was attending California State University Northridge (CSUN) and lived in the campus dorms. He agreed to let me spend a few weeks with him until I found something permanent. CSUN was only about 30 minutes from Pepperdine; my drive to school in the mornings was no longer stressful, and I could stay on campus as late as I needed.

A few weeks into the semester, I found a room to rent for $1,000 in Northridge, about 30 minutes from Pepperdine's campus. While I had scholarship money to pay for tuition, I now needed more money for rent; I didn't earn enough through my campus jobs to pay for rent, utilities, and other expenses. Fortunately, Winston agreed to loan me $3,000 for the semester. His continued kindness and support were always baffling to me. I did not understand why he gave so much to me – his time, his support, and his finances – but he did, and I was grateful. Our agreement stated that once I started making money, I would pay him back with interest.[4]

During the second semester of the first year, I applied for an internship with the Louisiana Department of Education and was chosen to spend three months in Baton Rouge for the summer of 2014. I also applied to be a graduate assistant with the intercultural affairs office in which I would work with undergraduate students and multicultural clubs and plan events on campus. The assistantship also included graduate student housing on campus and a meal plan. I was chosen and began the assistantship in the fall.

During the fall of my second and final year, I lived on campus so I did not have to worry about commuting. My assistantship paid for my housing and food. My job at Jamba Juice gave me the additional income I needed. I had my needs met, but I still lacked community. There were no graduate BSU or DREAMers organizations on campus. It is not uncommon to not have student organizations for graduate students, but as a Black undocumented student, an organization or a group was what I needed to feel a sense of belonging and community. And while I had shared my undocumented status with Winston, it was still a big secret from everyone else, so a safe space felt necessary. Unfortunately, an organized space on campus did not exist.

Professor Jones was a law professor at Pepperdine Law School, and his wife was a professor in the School of Psychology. I met him at the law library on campus. He was the only Black male professor at the law school at the time, so I knew about him through the conversations I heard the law students having. One day, Professor Jones came up to me and asked if I was a 1L (a first year law student). I told him I was a student in the School of Public Policy but had always dreamt of going to law school. He sat by me that day, and we began talking. Professor Jones and I talked for about 20 minutes every day after that first day we met. He eventually invited me to his house for a Sunday Bible study and dinner. The weekly Sunday Bible study and dinner event was a highly coveted invite that all the law students wanted. But, Professor Jones only invited a few students, mostly 2LS or 3Ls (second- and third-year law students), and I was now in that group. The first time I went to Professor Jones' house, I was struck by the extravagance of it all. His house was located in Malibu, on the top of a hill, about a mile from Pepperdine's campus. There were no other houses within blocks of his. As soon as I drove up to his gateway, I saw an infinity pool, four different barbeque grills, and many lounge chairs. As I entered the house, I noticed the tall ceilings, the granite countertops, the huge couches. His house was one you see in the movies. I was in awe. I attended the Bible study every Sunday, in part to admire the house. But I did enjoy the Bible study because it gave me an opportunity to explore my faith and my relationship with God, one that I was redefining over the years.

In that group, I had a sense of community. The students were all invested in developing their faith and redefining what faith meant to them. I was also grateful for this Bible study group because I met one of my closest friends, Adrian Dapper. Adrian was a Black man, well-dressed, and had a very comedic wit about him. He was also a student in the Public Policy program.

We instantly connected on the fact that we were the only two Public Policy students at Professor Jones' Bible study. We also bonded because we both grew up in Inglewood, CA; he could relate to the struggles of being Black on a predominantly white campus. Adrian and I would often talk about our hopes and dreams for the future, our deepest desires, and the hope our faith gives us to keep moving forward. Eventually, we also found out that we both were Momentum Millennium scholars. Our connection provided me with a sense of community.

By my second semester of my second year, I was well adjusted. I had figured out how to persevere through many challenges, in large part due to my faith and the kindness of others. I had gotten accustomed to the rigor of the work, and my basic needs were met. Additionally, my new connection with Adrian and the mentorship from Professor Jones were pivotal in my persistence. However, I was still burdened by and ashamed of my undocumented status, a feeling that stayed with me for many more years to come.

Soon, it was time for graduation.

A month or so before graduation, Professor Jones and his wife asked how I would celebrate the accomplishment. I told them I was not sure, but I wanted to celebrate because I missed that opportunity two years before. The next day, I got an email from his wife stating that she would love it if I had a celebration at their house. We agreed that I could invite 30 people, and I could have the space for four hours after graduation. It was such a grand gesture from two people I had only met a few months prior.

Adrian and I had a joint celebration, and I invited a few friends from middle and high school and from Cal Lutheran for my graduation and graduation party. On April 17, 2015, I graduated from Pepperdine University with a master's degree in Public Policy, at the top of my class. I enjoyed the moment as much as I could; I listened to all the speakers, paid attention to everyone who was present, took pictures with all my guests, and I smiled in every picture. It was a redo of 2013, but this time, I got it right.

After the ceremony, I celebrated at my party at Professor Jones' house. While the next step was unclear, since I graduated without a job and direction, that day was reserved for a celebration. I was now a newly crowned Master of Public Policy, an accomplishment bigger than me.

Notes

The stories that are told in this chapter are from my perspective and could be interpreted differently by others. To protect the identity of my family and friends, some names used in this chapter are pseudonyms.

1. A score of 160 or above is considered a good score.

2. Undocumented students still don't have access to federal aid in 2023.
3. Undocumented immigrants are not able to travel abroad because of their immigrant status. There are exceptions with Advance Parole.
4. This loan is still acquiring interest, as Winston has yet to ask for it. I should probably just offer to pay him back.

4

BLACK, UNDOCUMENTED, AND SUCCESSFUL?

After graduating from Pepperdine, I was on a high because I did the unimaginable; I had a master's degree.[1] I was in elite company, but I did not know what was next. Uncertainty seemed to be a consistent theme after my graduations. But I remained in good spirits. My main goal for the summer of 2015 was to secure a job, a task that was gruesome, but I was up for the challenge. I searched for policy jobs and did not find anything. Eventually, I shifted my search to jobs in education but still did not find anything. Soon, I started looking for jobs at universities, but I could not find anything. It was as if I had been on a rocky boat ride for the last two years, and even though I landed safely, I did not have a map to guide me to my next destination.

Eventually, I moved in with Winston and hit a low point. I had two degrees but no job. I was a newly crowned Master of Public Policy sleeping on my best friend's couch.

This was a three-peat. Where did I go wrong?

In July 2015, I found an ad for an AmeriCorps service opportunity at Great Oaks Charter School in Wilmington, Delaware. The opportunity would be for one year and included a $12,000 stipend, free housing, and a $6,000 education grant upon completion of the year-long fellowship. However, there was a citizenship requirement. As a graduate student, I had applied for the Momentum Millennium scholarship, which also had a citizenship requirement, and they made an exception for me. My hope was that the AmeriCorps program would do the same. While I was not excited about the possibility of moving thousands of miles away from the only place I had known in America, considering the alternative – homeless and unemployed – I applied for the position. Within a day of applying, I was interviewed and was offered the

DOI: 10.4324/9781003442998-5

role. But, there was a caveat. I would not get a $12,000 stipend because I did not meet the citizenship requirement, and AmeriCorps is a federally funded program; instead, the school that I would be placed at would pay me $7,500 directly. Additionally, I would not get the education grant that would be awarded to my peers, even after completing the year of service. To make matters worse, while I would still be in the AmeriCorps cohort for 2015, I would not officially be an AmeriCorps member on paper. It was a blow from all angles, and my undocumented status was the cause. During that time, I held Jeremiah 29:11 close, and out of desperate need, I accepted the position. I needed a job, and I wanted to get out of Winston's apartment; I felt like a continuous burden to him. With the last of my money, I flew to Wilmington, Delaware, to start my education fellowship with Great Oaks Charter School.

Great Oaks Charter School is a network of schools with locations in Wilmington, Delaware; Bridgeport, Connecticut; Newark, New Jersey; and Brooklyn, New York. Their mission is to provide individualized tutoring to students in preparation for them to be college-ready. In my role as an urban education fellow, which was really just a fancy way of saying I was a tutor, I would be working at the newest location in Wilmington with sixth-grade students.

When I got to the airport in Philadelphia, I was greeted by Kirstie, the Fellowship Director, who would also be my boss for the next few years. She was a white woman with red hair and a very perky attitude. She spoke energetically about Great Oaks and what she planned to do as a leader. She also told me that my apartment was located in downtown Wilmington, and it was only a five-minute walk from the job. I was grateful that she picked me up from the airport and that she allowed me to move into the apartment a week before the start date, which she agreed to because I shared that I was unhoused.

Within 30 minutes or so, we pulled up to the Residences at Rodney Square, my new home. My apartment was on the seventh floor. It was a one-bedroom apartment with wood floors and huge windows in the living room and the bedroom. There were two twin-sized beds in the bedroom; one would be for me and the other for my roommate. I was not excited to share a room with another adult at 23 years old, but this was my new reality and I had to adjust.

Great Oaks was located on the eighth floor of the Community Education Building (CEB) in downtown Wilmington; Kirstie was right, the walk from my apartment was only five minutes. Without a car, the commute was exactly what I needed.

Within two weeks, I would meet 36 other tutors; we would be the 2015–2016 AmeriCorps cohort.

As a tutor, I was a quick stand out. Kirstie gravitated to my work ethic, and other administrators in the school were impressed with my teaching abilities. After about two months at Great Oaks, the executive director, Kara, requested a meeting with me. Kara was high-spirited, brilliant, and very personable. She had a way with people and could easily draw anyone in. One of my colleagues once described her as someone who could sell water to a slug. In the meeting, Kara disclosed that she would like to hire me for the 2016–2017 school year as a social studies teacher. It was a great honor. However, while I thrived with planning my lessons for the students, enjoyed mingling my coworkers, and developed a reputation of being very strict, yet engaging, I did not like teaching. Teaching young students did not bring me joy, and I needed to honor that feeling even if it meant turning down a personalized offer. However, instead of rejecting the offer, I told her that I saw something else for myself at Great Oaks; I told her I could see myself developing a college counseling curriculum for the students. The idea had come to me because of the mission of the school, which was grounded on college access. Kara was impressed and told me she would follow up in the new year if she had room in the budget for such a position.

However, Kara did not let her idea of me teaching go very easily. Over the next few months, she would frequently visit my classroom and give me many compliments. She even shared her vision with other administrators who would jokingly say to me in the hallways, '*Can't wait to see you as a teacher next year*'. Their belief in me was encouraging. Still, I had no desire to be a teacher. Kara would challenge me all year to consider it, and every time, I politely declined the offer. Eventually, Kara made it clear that even if I did not want to be a teacher, she wanted to keep me at Great Oaks; she saw talent in me.

Kara and I revisited the college counseling curriculum conversation in December 2015, where she told me there was no budget for a position like the one I envisioned, but there might be an opening to support Kirstie in managing the AmeriCorps program. Kirstie was leading 37 people on her own that year, and it was taxing and unsustainable. She needed help. Kara thought I could help, and I did too. We were in agreement.

By this time, Kirstie and I had developed a strong relationship. Kirstie valued my insights about the program. Specifically, she liked my ideas on professional development, curriculum development, and the connection I had to the other tutors because of my relatable yet firm demeanor. She also valued that I had a master's degree; I was the only AmeriCorps member with one.

That same year, I was offered a $37,000 salary to manage the Ameri-Corps program alongside Kirstie. It was a unique position; I was not quali-fied to be an AmeriCorps member because of my immigrant status, but it was appropriate for me to manage the program. The strangeness of it did not deter me. It would be the first time I knew what my next steps would be after the close of a year, and that was the win I needed. Not to mention the salary was a step up from the $7,000 I had been earning the year prior. I started as the new AmeriCorps Manager in the summer of 2016.

That year, I worked to support Kirstie in managing the new AmeriCorps cohort of over 50 new college graduates, an increase from the previous year. Managing the new AmeriCorps members was surreal because I was leading young people. A year prior, I was just happy to have a place to live. But now, other young adults looked up to me. My new role was rewarding because the cohort gravitated to my matter-of-fact personality. Additionally, I developed a liking for coaching and managing people; it came naturally to me, and it was a skill that Kirstie and Kara nurtured. The job was also frustrating because while I was good at coaching the AmeriCorps members, I was not passionate about working in a middle school. The environment felt like the wrong fit, but I did not have the capacity or the luxury to explore purpose or passion.

Additionally, since I was still undocumented, I was paying close attention to the upcoming elections and was fearful that Donald Trump could assume the presidency. During his campaign, Trump had been very vocal about his disdain for immigrants. He called immigrants 'rapists' and 'drug dealers'. He was very adamant about his desires to build a wall, but he also noted that he would not 'touch' DREAMers.

On election night, I watched the results closely, knowing what it could mean for my future. Trump would go on to win one battleground state after another, and the next morning, Hilary Clinton conceded, stating, 'Our constitutional democracy enshrines the peaceful transition of power. We don't just respect that; we cherish it'. Her words were somber and painful for me, and I was completely terrified about what this new reality meant for my future. That day, I unconsciously wore all black to work; so did 90% of teachers, staff, administrators, and students. We were all at a loss for words. Students were concerned about what it meant for their parents, and they were especially saddened by Trump's election. I could not perform my duties that day.

Prior to Trump's election, I disclosed my DACA status to Kirstie, and she was very supportive. Before I saw her the morning after the election, she sent me a text: 'We won't let anything happen to you. We will hide you in our house if we have to'. She was joking about hiding me in her home, but it was a thoughtful text to receive from my supervisor. She cared about me. Uncle Shawn and Pastor Chaney also reached out via text, another show of support. However, after Trump's election, I felt the need to share my undocumented status with Kara. She had been very supportive about my professional growth, and I wanted her to be aware that I was undocumented. When I told Kara, she, too, was reassuring. My community was expanding.

In January 2017, Trump assumed office, and on September 5, 2017, he announced a plan to phase out DACA, a contrast from the promise he made on his campaign trail. His announcement prompted constant legal battles over DACA and sent my life into perpetual limbo. However, his presidency also sparked a knowing inside of me: *I was not happy.* Sure, I was growing as a young professional, and I would soon transition into a new role, Director of College Access; Kara had found the money in the budget. It was all coming to fruition. But, there was a constant whisper of unfulfillment. The lack of happiness came from an internal knowing: *I wanted to learn more about Black undocumented people and their experiences, but I was scared to be public about my own story.*

In early 2017, I began researching PhD and Ed.D. programs. I had also published an anonymous piece on the National Immigration Law Center website, sharing my story as a Black undocumented immigrant, my experiences navigating higher education, and the benefits of DACA. I was not ready to share my story publicly, but I was ready to do it anonymously. One step at a time, I thought.

During that time, I would also meet a new member of my community who would be instrumental for years to come.

In 2017, we welcomed the third AmeriCorps cohort, this time containing over 60 members. On the first day of training, Harper walked in, blue eyes, slim, with a great smile. She made a joke about the riveting information she had to read before signing a year of her life away to AmeriCorps. I laughed. I used her joke on other members throughout that day. We immediately became friends, and within a year, we were closer than ever.

I eventually told Harper about my DACA status. She was very understanding. With every person I shared my undocumented status with, it was like a continuous shedding of pounds, and if they responded kindly, it gave me more courage to continue sharing. Telling Harper I was undocumented was a big step for me. I never wanted anyone to think they could help me change my status, and I did not want them to shoulder that burden. But, with Harper, it felt safe. Similar to Winston, Harper would encourage me to go after all my dreams.

With Harper's encouragement and my desire, I latched on to the idea that I could go back to school. I had already been thinking about doctorate programs, but I did not have the confidence to apply. Additionally, applying to PhD programs would mean resigning from my full-time job, a luxury I could not afford.

However, the confidence began to grow with all of my professional success and the support of my community. So in 2018, I applied to one program: Temple University. In my personal statement, I shared about being an undocumented immigrant. Additionally, I made it clear that I wanted to learn more about the experiences of undocumented students within higher education. While I did not know what that meant for a career, I knew it was a deep calling in my soul that had been gnawing at me for years. It was another step toward owning my story and not being afraid.

Applying only to one program was a bold move, considering I did not have the best of luck applying to top programs, but Temple felt right. The university was located in Philadelphia, only about 30 minutes away from Harper's and my apartment. Additionally, I had extensive conversations with faculty who really wanted me to come on board. The faculty also shared about the rigor of the academics that I would delve into. Along with convenience of location, academics, and the potential support of faculty, Kara also made a commitment that Great Oaks would support my education financially if I committed to a program that would still ensure I was working at Great Oaks. Harper also promised financial support. In early 2019, I received my acceptance letter, and I committed to Temple University in the fall of 2019. With my acceptance letter also came a waiver to forgo some of the required classes because my master's degree met some of the requirements. This ensured that I could complete coursework in two years, if I attended as a full-time student.

As with my previous experience in higher education, I faced many significant barriers because I did not have access to in-state tuition, state financial aid, or other federal sources of support.[2] At Temple, I could not access reduced rates; I was classified as an international student, which meant that I would pay higher tuition fees. I was also ineligible for state financial aid as an undocumented student.

Additionally, committing to Temple as a full-time doctoral student with a full-time job was laborious. I no longer had free time because of my nightly commute to classes, weekends in the library, and late nights. I was operating on empty at all times.

However, even with the difficulty of balancing coursework, the dissertation process, and my personal life, this time around, as a doctoral student, I had more tools to navigate higher education. I knew how to talk to professors. I knew why I was there, and my community had grown in support. For the next two years, Harper would play a major role in ensuring I navigated successfully. She served as my personal editor for all my papers, and she even supported me financially. Kara kept her promise as well and gave me a stipend as a part of my job contract with Great Oaks to develop independent college counseling content. Additionally, I had a professor who really helped me persist. Dr. Daley was an Associate Professor in Temple's Higher Education program. He was engaging, funny, understanding, and vocal about his support for me. When I first met Dr. Daley, he shared his support and intrigue about my potential research topic. He saw it as a unique one;

he had not known of others studying that exact topic. Dr. Daley would serve as my personal advisor and supporter throughout the program.

On January 11, 2020, a 53-second clip of me telling my story was published on the PBS website. That video changed my life because it was another step toward telling my story boldly. Prior to that, I had shared my story with members of my community in essays and anonymously through op-eds, but I was still hiding. However, with my permission, Dr. Daley played the PBS video in class. It was frightening, but I embraced it. On my drive home from school that night, I told Harper that it was the first time I realized that I can't hide and tell my story at the same time; I have to tell it bravely. From that moment, I began to tell my story as Felecia S. Russell. I was no longer sharing it through pseudonyms. It freed me.

Soon, the COVID-19 pandemic hit, and our classes transitioned online. The transition to online was bittersweet because I no longer had to commute to Philadelphia, but I missed being in person. I had to work extremely hard to maintain strong relationships with my professors and keep up with my coursework.

During that time, I also started getting invitations to speak at conferences and at universities. In the span of a few months, I spoke at Delaware State University, Cornell University, Rutgers University, Harvard, and many more prominent universities. People found my story fascinating. They saw me as someone who defied the odds. They were right, but I always reminded them that at every step of the way, there were people who were willing to lend a hand to me. With every speech, every conference, every workshop, and every conversation I had with another undocumented person, I wanted to emphasize the power of a supportive community.[3]

I also determined my dissertation topic. Initially, I wanted to understand the experiences of undocuBlack students within higher education. The topic expanded to exploring how salient identities (Black and undocumented) affect the way undocuBlack students experience college. The goal of that question was positioned to explore the intersections of identities (race and status) and provide higher education leaders, policymakers, and the undocumented community with insight about the undocuBlack community.

In the summer of 2021, I completed my coursework and applied for doctoral candidacy. I was elevated and approved to study: *The Invisibility of Undocumented Black Students within Higher Education and the Undocumented Community*. It was a monumental achievement, but it was accompanied by various new transitions.

In the summer of 2020, I transitioned from Great Oaks to Cristo Rey Philadelphia High School as the new Director of College and Career Counseling. It was a tough decision to make, leaving the school I had been at for five years, where I started my professional journey, but I had reached my ceiling. I worked remotely for Cristo Rey for an entire year. During that same year, Harper and I decided to end our apartment lease. She would be moving back to Iowa and I, back to California.

With my completed coursework, elevated candidacy, and new upcoming relocation to California, I also decided to resign from Cristo Rey the summer of 2021. I had known for a while that working in a middle or high school was not my passion, but I had grown to love parts of it: coaching, mentoring, and serving as an example for the students I served. But it was time to fully listen to the calling in my soul. The decision to move back to California after six years of being on the East Coast was strange. Living in Delaware had given me my wings, new dreams, and new hope, but it was time to revisit my roots, and I had the tools now to grow and bloom.

That summer, Harper and I drove cross country back to California. I moved in with Uncle Shawn and his family while I completed my dissertation. I also got an adjunct teaching position at Cal Lutheran. It was a full circle moment to walk into a classroom at Cal Lutheran as the professor. I could not believe that I was in the same classrooms I was in just ten years before, but this time, I was the teacher. I cherished every moment. I started every class the way Dr. Taylor started the summer class I took in 2010 – *Tell me who you are and what makes you you.* That same summer, I met up with Dr. Taylor for lunch and shared with him the impact that assignment had on me. We were now colleagues.[4]

I also started a full-time position as the Director of Undergraduate Admission at Cal Lutheran. My life was falling into place. While I was busy conducting my research, managing a team, and teaching, it was exactly what I needed to distract me from all the changes I had encountered within the year. As the holidays approached, I was grateful to have a safe place to rest my head each night, a job I enjoyed, and participants for my dissertation study. The year was coming to a good end. I was months away from being minted as Dr. Russell.

However, the start of 2022 was not so favorable.

In January 2022, grandma was diagnosed with stage 4 cancer. At that time, she had been living in Jacksonville, Florida, for five years. She was a permanent resident. While Mama lived in Florida, I visited her only once, a truth I am ashamed of. Within a week of her diagnosis, I made my way to Florida. From the moment she was diagnosed, I could barely write, read, eat, or sleep. My dissertation was on pause. Just a few months prior to visiting my grandma, my therapist had asked me, 'What is your biggest fear?' I had told her, 'That my grandmother will die in Jamaica, and I won't be able to attend the funeral'. My grandmother was now on her deathbed, and I had the chance to visit her; I was grateful. I remember walking into the hospital room and seeing her laying there, no longer the strong woman I knew. She smiled when she saw me,

'Wingin, a yuh dat?' she said with frailty.
'Yea, mama, a mi'.

We both teared up. She asked me to pray for her.

'Yuh still know how fi pray, right?'

I laughed.

'Yea mi nuh how fi pray'.

I prayed with her.

I spent a week in Florida with my grandmother as she was dying. Mommy and my siblings also got to be there. That week was not only difficult but also memorable. Grandma made everyone laugh and would recall stories of me waking up before her and demanding we do devotions. She even said I was steps ahead of her on Saturday mornings for church. Her stories gave me a foundation to understand my current work ethic and my own connection to faith and God. To this day, I still do my morning devotions. They don't look like they did when I did them with Mama, no songs or kneeling, but they still include scripture and prayer.

Within three weeks after being diagnosed, Grandma flew back to Jamaica with one of her sons. She had to travel in a wheelchair with her own oxygen tank, but she wanted to be back in Jamaica; she wanted to be around her family.

Grandma died on February 25, 2022, just a few weeks after she arrived back in Jamaica. She died peacefully in one of her daughter's house. I could not attend the funeral because of my immigration status.[5] Mommy and I watched the livestream together in her new apartment. I wept unbearably on the day of her funeral. My grandma was gone.

A few days after her funeral, I attempted to revisit my dissertation. I started small; I wrote an acknowledgment section and dedicated it to my grandma. That helped. Fortunately, one of the best lessons my grandmother taught me was to always value routine. So I began to slowly attempt to follow my daily routine. With her strength and my routine, I was back on track. Mama raised me to value education, work ethic, and my relationship with God; without the foundation she laid, I wouldn't be who I am today.

I successfully defended my dissertation on March 24, 2022, and graduated from Temple University in April of that same year. Harper, Winston, my nieces, and nephews were in attendance. I graduated from Temple University with a doctorate degree, an accomplishment only 1% of the population can claim.

On that day, I reflected.

I asked myself, *how did I make it?* The answer is clear, I had opportunities. In the small villages of Jamaica, in the neighborhoods of Compton, in the rural areas of Iowa, and the lone village in Nairobi, there is talent, but opportunity does not exist in all of those places. I made it to Cal Lutheran, partly because of my hard work, but so many other students work hard, so what was different? In high school, Mr. Tovar and Ms. Green were my advocates and believers, and they fought for me. In college, there was Uncle Shawn, Mark Warren, Dr. Sebastian Taylor, Dr. Moren, and many others. I had a best friend who always saw fit to help me, whether financially or personally; he showed up for me, especially at Pepperdine. At Temple, I had Harper, Dr. Daley, and scholarships. And before all of those angels, my mother made the tough decision to immigrate so her children could have a better life.

As famous rapper Big Sean said, 'With all the drive in the world, you still need gas'. I had the drive, and others gave me the gas. As you read the stories in the following chapters, you will see that without community, undocuBlack students had a harder time persisting, but with community, they had the fuel to keep going. While I am proud of my accomplishments, it is the brave 15 who decided to share their stories with me for my dissertation that I am most proud of. Not only is my story relevant for this work, but so are theirs.

References

American Immigration Council and Presidents' Alliance on Higher Education and Immigration. (2023). (rep.). *Undocumented students in higher education how many students are in U.S. colleges and universities, and who are they?* Retrieved from www.higheredimmigrationportal.org/research/undocumented-students-in-higher-education-updated-march-2021/.

Pennsylvania–data on immigrant students: Higher Ed immigration portal. Presidents' Alliance on Higher Education & Immigration. (2023, August 16). Retrieved from www.higheredimmigrationportal.org/state/pennsylvania/.

Notes

The stories that are told in this chapter are from my perspective and could be interpreted differently by others. To protect the identity of my family and friends, certain names used in this chapter are pseudonyms.

1. According to a report by the American Immigration Council and the Presidents' Alliance on Higher Education and Immigration, in 2021, it was estimated that 12.8% of undocumented students were enrolled in graduate programs.

2. According to the Higher Education Immigration Portal, Pennsylvania is classified as a limited state in terms of inclusive in-state tuition and state financial aid policies for undocumented students; this means policies provide the state's undocumented students, including DACA recipients, with access to in-state or reduced tuition in at least some public institutions.

3. In fact, while writing this book, I asked Uncle Shawn what I was like during this time, and he noted,

   [A]t the end of her high school term, Felecia seemed to be without hope and lived in fear; fear of telling anyone that she was undocumented, fear of deportation, and trying to stay hidden in society. What seemed to keep her going was an unrelenting belief that God walked along with her on her life journey. After graduation from California Lutheran University, she was hopeful and somewhat confident, but still was quite hesitant to tell anyone of her legal status. After getting her master's degree, Felecia was frustrated because she thought the degrees would be her golden ticket. Finally, after successfully working hard for five years and earning her doctorate, Felecia was confident, fully determined to tell her story, and equally determined to help those who had similar backgrounds. While the future of DREAMers are still uncertain and looms heavy in the back of one's mind, Felecia's faith continues to keep her full of hope and relentless in her pursuit to help others.

4. He is also a close friend.

5. I hope to visit her gravesite one day and share this book with her.

PART - 2

5

UNDOCUBLACK IMMIGRANT EXPERIENCES WITHIN THE CONTEXT OF HIGHER EDUCATION

In 2021, I interviewed 15 undocuBlack immigrants who were navigating higher education or had recently graduated from an institution of higher learning. To honor their stories, I created a profile of all the participants, detailing their backgrounds and their experiences. The positioning of their stories is presented through the lens of access and the hope of higher education. This approach is due in part to the barriers that undocumented immigrants face in accessing higher education but also to present the cultural embodiment of the importance of higher education engulfed in Black immigrant cultures. Therefore, even with the compounded barriers to higher education, Black immigrants continue to have high educational achievement. In 2019, according to the Pew Research Center, over 31% of Black immigrants held a bachelor's degree, which reflected a faster growth rate than any other population within the United States. (Tamir, 2022). Many scholars have argued as to why Black immigrants within the United States have demonstrated achievement differences, especially when thinking of U.S.-born Blacks (Ogbu, 1991; Ogbu & Simons, 1998). However, those theories will not be examined here, as the goal of the current study is not to demonstrate the educational differences among U.S.-born Blacks and Black immigrants, but to show that undocuBlack immigrants are continually persisting throughout education even with the barriers they face.

To protect the participants, I use pseudonyms in place of their given names. Additionally, I disguise all other markers of individual identification. The participants represented 11 different origin countries and 10 U.S. states. There were six self-identified males and nine self-identified females. At the time of the interviews, six were still pursuing their undergraduate studies, and nine had already graduated college; of the nine, four were pursuing graduate degrees.

DOI: 10.4324/9781003442998-7

Their stories, presented in this chapter, represent grit, resiliency, and cultural norms.

Abraham Brace

> *I mean, for me, I was good at school. . . . I didn't have other talents so school became it.*

Abraham immigrated from Senegal to the United States when he was 14 years old. He grew up in New York. At the time of the interview, he was 26 years old and had already completed his bachelor's and master's degrees.

Similar to some of the other participants, Abraham understood that he was undocumented when he attempted to get a driver's license but realized he was ineligible for one. He described his initial experiences after he found out as, '*a lot of hiding, a lot of lying, a lot of shaming . . . I was always afraid*'.

Nonetheless, Abraham wanted a better life for himself, and he saw education as a path to that life. When asked why he pursued college, he replied, '*I mean, for me, I was good at school. I don't have talent. I was not a good athlete, so I'll just continue my education and get some skills, so that's what made me go to college*'. Additionally, Abraham had the support of his family to pursue higher education, which helped him along the way; according to Abraham, the support of his family was pivotal.

Yet, Abraham's higher education trajectory was still very arduous as he navigated the educational system as an undocumented person without access to DACA. After high school, he enrolled at a local community college because he could not access state or federal aid, and he was not aware of any scholarships for undocumented students. After a few years of community college, Abraham transferred to a four-year institution in Mississippi[1] where he completed his bachelor's degree. During this time, Abraham had to work to fund his education; he had different 'under the table' jobs to provide a source of income.[2] Abraham went on to earn his master's degree in 2021. For Abraham, college was never a question; it was always the answer.

Anthony Esmine

> '*Number one it's pretty much what we do at home, and I have always wanted to be a doctor*'.

Anthony was born in Nigeria and immigrated to the United States when he was 18 years old, without his immediate family. At the time of the interview, he was in his second year of community college and hoped to transfer to a four-year institution and eventually graduate.

Once Anthony was in the United States, he applied for a student visa, but the application was rejected. Soon, he realized this meant he was classified as undocumented. He described that his initial feelings were mainly rooted in fear because he did not know what it meant for his life in America. Nonetheless, he still pursued higher education because it was all he knew. According to Anthony,

> *When it comes to college education, it's a necessity — that's how we see it in our family. My dad is an accountant, and my mother is a nurse. A college education is a big thing in my family, and they are the reason why I'm still here. So even when I wanted to give up, they always encouraged me to keep going.*

Because of his family's beliefs and their support, Anthony knew he had to still pursue higher education, even if it would be difficult as an undocumented person.

Anthony enrolled at the local community college as an undocumented student with no prior schooling experience in the United States. After three semesters at the community college, he learned about the DREAM Center[3] on his campus. Fortunately, through the center, he found community and access to resources. The DREAM Center became his place of refuge as he learned about financial resources and applying for identification. He also had access to Immigrants Rising,[4] where he learned about applying for an ITIN number. However, he still struggled to pay for his education. Anthony shared,

> *I struggled to pay the tuition fees, because it is high, and I don't have a job. Just my dad from Nigeria, sending me money, but the dollar rate is so terrible, it was hard for him to do it. But, if I ask for financial support, I get it from them.*

Even with the financial challenges that he faced, higher education was a goal that Anthony was not willing to forego.

Arion Dirk

> *After my son was born, I realized I needed to go to school. We became homeless.*

Arion was born in Jamaica and immigrated to the United States when he was ten years old. He grew up in South Central Los Angeles with his immediate family: his mother, three sisters, and one older brother. At the time of the interview, he was 28 years old and in his final year of his undergraduate career. He is also a DACA recipient.

When Arion was in high school, he learned that he was undocumented because he could not access a driver's license; in this way, his story was similar to other participants. As Arion described his experience of understanding his immigration status, he noted feeling lonely and wanting to give up. He stated, '*I think I gave up. I thought there was nothing else for me. I thought I couldn't go to school, and I wouldn't be able to get a job, so what's the point?*' Even so, he kept moving forward.

After he graduated from high school, he enrolled in a local community college. However, he struggled to keep up with his schoolwork because of family responsibilities. Arion served as a main support for his mother, who was also undocumented. After one semester of community college, Arion stopped so that he could support his family. Over the next four years after high school, he reenrolled at community colleges many different times, but he could never persist because of extenuating circumstances.

When asked why he pursued a college degree, he stated,

> *After my son was born, I realized I needed to go to school. We became homeless. My son was sleeping in the car. I needed to go to school to give my son a better life. I need to do something better with my life, and I need to give him a better life, so I need to go to school, and that's when I started.*

Unlike most Black immigrants in this study, Arion did not have the initial support of his family. His family needed to survive, and he assumed the role of provider. Yet, Arion knew he now needed to provide for his son, and he believed a college degree would help to improve their lives.

After the birth of his son, he reenrolled at another community college, but this time performing at a higher level with his son as his motivation.

During those years, Arion maintained a high academic standing and was eventually able to transfer to a private four-year university where he received a full-tuition scholarship based on his prior academic achievement. He was scheduled to graduate in May 2022. For Arion, higher education was a vehicle to upward mobility.

Darius Major

> *I didn't really have an option; it was my dream.*

Darius was born in Trinidad and immigrated to the United States when he was nine years old. He is a DACA recipient. At the time of the interview, he was 28 years old, living in Pennsylvania – the state he grew up in and calls his home.

Unlike many of the other undocuBlack immigrants I interviewed, Darius was aware that he was undocumented from a young age because his mother told him. While he understood that he was undocumented, he still did not know what it meant and how it would later affect his life. While he was in high school, he felt secluded and fearful because he could not tell anyone about his immigration status.

Darius knew that he wanted to go to college. He said,

I didn't really have an option. It was always my dream. I wanted to be a lawyer, but I had to give it up. For Caribbean folks, it is either doctor or lawyer, but I have given up on my dream to be a lawyer.

Darius enrolled at a four-year public university with the support of his mother. They paid out of pocket for tuition and housing. Darius also worked two off-campus jobs to support his college education. While he had the support of his mother, he did not have other support structures in place. There were no organizations or student clubs on his campus for undocumented students, which led to him feeling isolated from his peers.

Darius' higher education journey was lonely and isolating because of the arduous and exhausting nature of navigating both his Blackness and his immigration status. However, both identities (Black and undocumented) motivated him to complete his coursework; he graduated from college in 2021. For Daris, college was his saving grace; he needed to make it.

Fatima Oli

I am from an African background and college is necessary.

Fatima immigrated from Nigeria at six years old and grew up in Georgia. She is a DACA recipient.

Fatima learned of her undocumented status when she wanted to get a driver's license and could not do so because she did not have a social security number. After learning of her undocumented status, she felt depressed and hopeless.

She wanted to go to college because higher education was normalized within her African culture. According to Fatima, '*It was just an understanding that I go to college even if I knew my mom could not afford it*'. Even though her family could not afford to pay for a college education, higher education was a necessary next step. However, Fatima knew she needed support if she was going to enroll in higher education, so she disclosed her immigration status to her high school counselor; according to Fatima, her

counselor was very supportive. He introduced her to TheDream.US[5] scholarship, which Fatima applied for and was awarded. With the scholarship, she
enrolled at an HBCU.

While in college, she maintained strong relationships with faculty, staff,
and administrators. These relationships were instrumental in her persistence. However, she did note that she did not have very good relationships
with other students as she was focused on her academics, working, and
building relationships with staff. The isolation from her peers motivated
her to work even harder in school. She also had an internship on campus,
which provided her with work experience. Finally, as a result of the full academic scholarship, she never worried about finances. Fatima was scheduled
to graduate with a bachelor's degree in May 2022. For Fatima, her education was her super power.

Gabby Neuman

> *I couldn't do anything else, so school, I say this all the time, like I don't even
> want to graduate school because it is all I have, so it's like what am I going
> to do when I graduate.*

Gabby was born in Kenya and immigrated to the United States with her
family when she was five years old. She grew up in Texas.

Gabby learned of her undocumented status as a sophomore in high
school when she could not get a driver's license. Similar to others, she felt
lonely, depressed, and defeated.

However, even with her undocumented status, Gabby knew she would
go to college because her family valued education. Fortunately, she had
strong grades, which earned her a full academic scholarship to a four-year
public university.

While in college, Gabby did not disclose her status to anyone out of
fear of being outed. She also noted that while her college campus offered
resources and support for undocumented students, those resources were
mainly for students with DACA status; as someone without DACA, she
felt even more isolated from the undocumented community. Additionally, she struggled to financially pay for school, often having to turn to
her family for support. As she recalls, '*They helped me financially, even
now, because I obviously can't work,*[6] *and they want me to focus 100% on
school, so they help me financially*'. Nonetheless, Gabby was persistent and
determined, graduating college in four years. At the time of the interview, she was pursuing a law degree. For Gabby, higher education was
always essential.

Greg Talib

For me, that's how it was. My mom was like, you have to go to college, you have to go to college, and even though she didn't understand how much of a barrier it would be, she still wanted it for me.

Greg was born in Togo, but his family immigrated to the United States when he was one-year old. He grew up in Utah with his immediate family. Greg is a DACA recipient. Greg graduated with a bachelor's degree in 2021; his college journey spanned five years.

Greg was aware of his undocumented status at a very young age because his mother told him about it. He worked hard with the desire that his hard work would be enough even with the burden of knowing he was undocumented.

When asked why he pursued higher education, he said,

For me, that's how it was, my mom was like you have to go to college, you have to go to college and even though she didn't understand how much of a barrier it would be, she still wanted it for me.

Attending college was an expectation from his family and his own understanding of his familial background and the importance they place on higher education. However, according to Greg, he did not aim very high when applying to college because he knew his family could not afford private schools without access to federal aid. He was accepted to his local public university, and with the support of his family, he enrolled.

While being a student at the university, he had access to a DREAM Center. Greg utilized the space for community and resources. He told the staff in that center about his status because there were no other support services on his campus. While he had support in the DREAM Center, he struggled to financially afford his college education. Greg stated,

My mom did a lot of stuff to help me pay for college. She was a part of this thing called banda, I don't know what they call it in English or whatever, but it's where a bunch of people pull their money together, and then every so often different people receive the bounty. She used that to pay for my school. Also, we lived in a smaller house with a much cheaper rent so we could have extra money to pay for school.

Greg's family was in total support of his pursuit of higher education and made it their mission to help him persist.

While Greg had some struggles, he eventually made it to the finish line and graduated with high academic honors. Greg credits his family for their financial, emotional, and mental support throughout his collegiate journey.

Lucy Ivette

So, my parents always told me that's what I was going to do, that I was going to go to school, I was going to be educated.

Lucy was born in Haiti, and her family immigrated to the United States when she was only nine months old. She grew up in Florida. At the time of her interview, she was 26 years old, and she had already graduated with her bachelor's degree and was concluding her first year as a PhD student at a public university.

When she was 13 years old, ICE agents raided Lucy's house and took her father. He was later deported back to Haiti. Lucy understood that she was undocumented after the raid and started to notice the significant differences between her and her peers. For instance, they could access a driver's license and after school jobs, but she was not able to acquire a job or a license because of her status. As a middle-school student, she felt lonely and isolated because of her status. However, Lucy had a deep desire to be a scientist, so she continued to work hard in school.

When asked why she pursued college, she noted,

Well, both my parents only have eighth grade education, so even as a kid they always told me that I was going to go to school and I had to get good grades. They very much instilled that in me.

Therefore, Lucy never questioned if she would attend college but how. As a high school senior, she shared her legal status with a teacher because she wanted to have all the information she needed to apply to college. Fortunately, the teacher was supportive and introduced her to the UndocuBlack Network.[7] The undocuBlack Network became a safe place for Lucy because she felt she had community. Everyone was Black, and they understood the intersections of race and status.

With the support of her family and the undocuBlack Network, she applied to colleges. She eventually enrolled at a local private college but struggled persisting because of cost and working multiple jobs. She then transferred to a public institution in hopes that she could afford tuition. While at the public institution, she worked two jobs while keeping up with her coursework. However, she continued to persist and eventually graduated. For Lucy, college was always on the table, and with the support of her family, teachers, and her own motivation, she approached higher education as a necessary road to success.

Mitch Monroe

I had a teacher and she was in the undocuBlack community. She made me realize it was possible to attend college. I did not know it was possible.

Mitch came to the United States from Gabon on a tourist visa while he was a sophomore in high school. He overstayed his visa, which transitioned him to undocumented status. Of all the participants, he was one of two who arrived in the United States during high school. At the time of the interview, Mitch was 20 years old and still undocumented. Mitch hoped to graduate from college in 2025 with a bachelor's degree.

Mitch did not understand that he was undocumented until he was a junior in high school. His undocumented status was revealed when he tried to get a summer job and a driver's license but was told he did not have the right documentation to do so. Mitch noted that he experienced loneliness, fear, and a constant need to hide his status from his friends. He recognized that he was frequently lying to others; it became second nature in order to protect himself. However, his high school science teacher was a member of the UndocuBlack Network, and she was very vocal about her immigration status. As a result, Mitch felt comfortable disclosing his status to her. His news was met with acceptance, and she helped him navigate the college application process. Before disclosing his status to his teacher, Mitch thought he could not go to college. He elaborates, '*My teacher told me it was possible. She gave me resources. My science teacher encouraged me to keep going so I applied with some good grades*'. Mitch was one of two participants who did not have the assumption that college was important. However, with the support of his teacher, higher education seemed like a reachable goal.

With the help of his teachers, he applied to several colleges. Mitch was awarded a full academic scholarship to a four-year HBCU. Mitch's college journey was largely positive because of his positioning at an HBCU and his access to a full academic scholarship. For Mitch, higher education will provide him with ample opportunities to create a better future for himself.

Rosemary Rundell

Two things: one, I was good at Science, and I liked it, and I wanted to continue, but then two, I felt like that was really my only option.

Rosemary was born in Jamaica and immigrated to the United States with her mother and younger sister when she was 11 years old. Rosemary grew up in Maryland.

Unlike many of the participants, she knew she was undocumented at an early age, which resulted in her being careful with all of her decisions. This meant she never allowed herself to go to parties or build relationships with others because she always feared encounters with police and did not want to jeopardize her future. Her immigration status created many mental barriers for her, including pursuing higher education. According to Rosemary, even with impeccable grades, she did not envision going to college because of her undocumented status. However, without DACA status, education seemed to be the only way to continue surviving, so Rosemary applied to colleges with hopes of becoming a scientist. As she noted, *'going to school would provide me with security'*.

After high school, Rosemary attended a local community college for two years and then transferred to a four-year university. While at the four-year institution, she had no support from faculty and staff because they were not informed on how to support her. As a result of the constant lack of support, she felt isolated from her peers and secluded herself from her campus community. Therefore, she navigated higher education without much community or support. However, Rosemary knew that education was her only option, so she continued to excel in her academics, while working several jobs to fund her education.

She graduated in 2021 with a bachelor's degree with the hopes of starting a PhD program. For Rosemary, while higher education had always been an expectation from her family, it became essential for her future.

Raven Reeves

> *Being low income my whole life, not only because of our citizenship status but also because my mom only got a high school education and even now, I'm still affected by it, I just knew that I didn't want that for myself.*

Raven was born in Jamaica and immigrated to the United States when she was eight years old. She grew up in Maryland.

Raven was unaware of her undocumented status because her mother did not disclose it to her out of fear that she might limit her own possibilities. Raven noted that she was grateful to not know that she was undocumented because she did not place any limits on her dreams. However, once she really understood what it meant to be undocumented, she felt discouraged, angry, confused, and doubtful.

Nonetheless, Raven wanted to go to college because she desired a better life for herself, so she applied to college. Eventually, she was awarded a sizable scholarship to attend her local four-year public institution. The university was in close proximity to her apartment, so she commuted. Raven's first year in college was 2020, at the height of COVID-19 pandemic. Raven struggled to foster relationships with other students because she commuted to campus and because the campus was operating remotely. Therefore, she noted that she was not sure what her sense of community would be like if she had the opportunity to live on campus and foster community. At the time of the interview, Raven was in her second year of her undergraduate journey. She planned to graduate with a bachelor's degree in 2024.

For Raven, college is an avenue to more opportunities.

Sasha Oscar

> *I had been working for families, and I knew that there had to be more. I honestly got tired.*

Sasha was born in Trinidad and immigrated to the United States when she was eight years old. She is a DACA recipient. She grew up in Pennsylvania.

Sasha has known about her undocumented status from a young age. Sasha thought that her undocumented status meant that she could not go to college, as she heard from her high school counselor that undocumented students could not attend college. Therefore, after graduating high school, Gabby worked many jobs to sustain her life.

However, in 2013, Sasha applied for DACA and enrolled at a local community college. During her time at the community college, she disclosed her status to her English professor. Her professor was very supportive. It took Sasha six years to graduate from the community college because she had no support system. She has no family in America, and she had to pay for school on her own. According to Sasha,

> *My family is complex if nothing else and complicated. They were supportive in ways that they could be. I think everybody just didn't really know the process, so a lot of it was me having to learn a lot of things on my own and even now like trying to explain the fact that I'm doing my bachelor's and my master's to my mom and my dad who still lives in Trinidad, it's very much like talking to a child.*

As Sasha notes, because her family is unfamiliar with the college process, she has had to figure out how to support herself.

She eventually enrolled at her local four-year university in a 4 + 1 program to earn a bachelor's and master's degree. She continued to work multiple jobs to afford her degree. Sasha hoped to graduate in 2024.

For Sasha, while college was not always an option, she is working hard to see this new dream come to fruition.

Shannon Avery

I think it was just a definite. It wasn't something I even questioned because for sure my mom is also somebody who's very studious.

Shannon was born in Kenya and came to the United States from Canada when she was 12 years old. She grew up in California.

After being in the United States for a few years, her visa expired. However, for many years, Shannon had no idea that the expiration of her visa meant that she was undocumented. Without an awareness of the gravity of her legal status, she navigated middle and high school without placing limitations on herself. According to Shannon, not realizing that she was undocumented was beneficial for her because she aimed high during her college search; had she understood what it meant to be undocumented, she would have altered her goals. For Shannon, college was always a possibility because her family valued education. She said, '*My mom was very supportive in always telling me to apply to college and figure out the rest later*'.

After being admitted to a university, Shannon was classified as an international student. Knowing she had been in the United States for many years and was cognizant of residency status, she inquired about why she was being classified as an international student. Through this process, she learned that she was undocumented. Once she understood what it meant to be undocumented, she felt lonely, fearful, and scared. Furthermore, she did not qualify for DACA, which added additional stress. Shannon decided to disclose her status to the administrators at her university, which caused tension with her mother. This decision left her alone without any familial support. Fortunately, she enrolled at a public four-year institution that had an Undocumented Student Resource Center (USRC), otherwise known as a DREAM Center. Shannon was very involved at the DREAM Center as a volunteer because she could not legally get a job. She eventually applied for fellowships to fund her education.

Her time in college was difficult because of the lack of access to funding, community, and familial support. She got very involved in advocacy to support students without DACA status, but her involvement made her grades suffer. According to Shannon, '*I think yeah the fact that I had to advocate a lot in order to get resources I need to survive definitely took a toll on my mental health*'. Therefore, she struggled to maintain her academic duties because she had to spend her time advocating. For Shannon, while college had always been expected of her, it was through her advocacy that she found her passion.

Teresa Moore

> '*Education was for my family, everyone is very highly educated. I thought this is the only route I envision for my life*'.

Teresa was born in Malawi and immigrated to the United States with her family when she was only two years old. She grew up in Indiana.

For Teresa, learning about her undocumented status was staggered. She first learned about it when she could not access a driver's license but did not fully understand the gravity of it until she could not fill out the FAFSA during her senior year of high school. During that time, she experienced feelings of unworthiness and doubt about her ability to attend college. She even felt depressed. However, her family was very adamant about a college education, so Teresa pushed through her uncertainty. According to Teresa,

> *There were times when I wanted to be a doctor, I wanted to be a ballerina, but all roads were leading to college. Like there's not a time in my life where I didn't think I was going to go to college. But, because of the depression, I waited until the last minute to apply for colleges.*

As a high school senior, she applied to many colleges but was not accepted by any of the institutions she applied to. She then decided to enroll at her local community college. After only one semester at the local community college, she dropped out because she was mentally exhausted. While she was out of school, she applied for DACA, which opened up doors for her. Once approved for DACA, Teresa returned to the community college and disclosed her status to her peers, staff, faculty, and administrators. She became a spokesperson for undocumented students. Even though Teresa was vocal about her status the second time around, she noted that there were no support services on her campus for undocumented students, which made her advocacy difficult.

At the time of the interview, Teresa had been at the community college for six years. She hoped to transfer to a four-year college within a year. For Teresa, a college education is required, and she will continue to fight for her place in higher education.

Taryn Hoover

> *I did not think I would go to college. My parents did not have the money.*

Taryn was born in Barbados and immigrated to the United States when she was 12 years old. She grew up in New York. She was a DACA recipient. At the time of the interview, she was 24 years old.

During the middle school, Taryn learned she was undocumented because she could not get New York state identification. After learning about her immigration status, she felt lonely; this knowledge also affected her academic performance. Prior to understanding her immigrant status, Taryn excelled in her academics, but the news about her status made her future seem bleak. She began performing poorly in school because she thought her college dreams were over. Fortunately, Taryn had a high school counselor she trusted and to whom she confided in about her status. The counselor was very motivating for Taryn, which gave her new hope. According to Taryn, once she found out she was undocumented, '*I did not think I would go to college. My parents did not have the money. I applied to scholarships and did not get them. My counselor motivated me. She was very invested*'. Additionally, Taryn's family was adamant about her getting a college education, so she continued to push forward in school, and with the help of her counselor and teachers, Taryn applied for college.

She enrolled at her local state university and commuted from home. As a commuter, Taryn did not have time to participate in student activities on campus, which isolated her from having relationships with students, faculty, and staff. Fortunately, she received a scholarship from TheDream.US, which provided her with a better opportunity to continue her education. However, even with finances covered, Taryn struggled academically, financially, and emotionally while in college. She recounted a heartbreaking experience, having to forfeit her Mandarin major because of a travel requirement. She stopped attending classes, was often depressed, and her cumulative undergraduate grade point average declined from a 3.5 to a 2.1. It was through the support of her family that she got back on track. Taryn graduated with a bachelor's degree in 2019.

Taryn considers herself fortunate because of TheDream.US scholarship, which made college a reality for her.

Summary

The 15 profiles explore the nature of the Black immigrant experience with higher education. Within Black immigrant culture, education is important. The persistence of the undocuBlack participants within the current study demonstrates the embedded culture of higher education.

While the participants all had different experiences with accessing higher education, they all shared similar struggles with success within higher education.

Notes

1. According to the higher education immigration portal, Mississippi does not provide undocumented residents with access to in-state tuition or state financial aid. DACA recipients do have access to in-state tuition in Mississippi, but Abraham did not have DACA.
2. Without DACA and a social security number, Abraham could not legally be employed.
3. '(USRCs) are institutionally supported physical structures on higher education campuses that provide access to opportunities for undocumented high school, transfer, undergraduate, and graduate students, as well as students from mixed-status families' (Cisneros & Valdivia, 2020, p. 52).
4. Founded in 2006, Immigrants Rising transforms individuals and fuels broader changes. With resources and support, undocumented people are able to get an education, pursue careers, and build a brighter future for themselves and their community.
5. TheDream.US scholarships are for highly motivated undocumented students who want nothing more than to get a college education but are unable to afford the cost. They have no access to federal aid, limited access to state aid, and they sometimes face paying out-of-state tuition.
6. Without DACA or a social security number, Gabby could not be legally employed.
7. The UndocuBlack Network is a multigenerational network of currently and formerly undocumented Black people that fosters community, facilitates access to resources, and advocates to transform the realities of Black immigrants.

References

Mississippi–data on immigrant students: Higher Ed immigration portal. Presidents' Alliance. (2023, August 16). Retrieved from www.higheredimmigrationportal. org/state/mississippi/.

Ogbu, J. (1991). Immigrant and involuntary minorities in perspective. In M. Gibson & J. Ogbu (Eds.), *Minority status and schooling: A comparative study of immigrant and involuntary minorities* (pp. 3–33). Garland.

Ogbu, J., & Simons, H. (1998). Voluntary and involuntary minorities: A cultural-ecological theory of school performance with some implications for education. *Anthropology & Education Quarterly, 29,* 155–188.

Tamir, C. (2022, February 1). *Key findings about black immigrants in the U.S.* Pew Research Center. Retrieved from www.pewresearch.org/short-reads/2022/01/27/key-findings-about-black-immigrants-in-the-u-s/.

6

SENSE OF BELONGING ON COLLEGE CAMPUSES FOR UNDOCUBLACK STUDENTS

Contextualizing the Sense of Belonging

To set the stage to discuss belonging, it is important to understand how belonging is defined and how it has been understood within higher education over the years. As my study is rooted in race and immigration, I provide various definitions of belonging and a glimpse of the literature on belonging within the context of race and immigration, such as belonging and racial identities, belonging and engagement, and belonging and undocumented students. Following, I lay out Strayhorn's (2012) definition of belonging and discuss why I center it within my study to frame the experiences of the undocuBlack participants. Then, I provide examples of the experiences of the undocuBlack participants within undocumented and Black spaces on their campuses and demonstrate how those experiences contributed to their sense of belonging, or lack thereof. Finally, the chapter concludes with a minor discussion on how we move forward.

Understanding of Belonging

Because numerous scholars have researched belonging, many definitions of belonging exist. For instance, Yuval-Davis (2011) defines a sense of belonging as a personal feeling of being included within a community. According to Yuval-Davis, belonging is really predicated on how someone feels. Hurtado and Carter (1997) assert that a sense of belonging is related to students' sense of connection, commonality, and positioning within the college community. In this case, belonging depends on

DOI: 10.4324/9781003442998-8

whether students see themselves represented and feel safe within spaces they should be able to occupy. In Tinto's (1993) study on student departure, he emphasized that students have to feel like they 'fit' within the university's systems, such as academics, campus activities, and campus environment, to feel a sense of belonging. He contends that if students are not able to integrate into those communities on campuses, they are less likely to persist.

Understanding the importance of belonging is necessary because scholars have asserted that belonging leads to successful persistence, academic success, and overall well-being (Hausmann et al., 2007; Tinto, 1993; Tovar et al., 2009). Conversely, not feeling a sense of belonging can result in a lack of engagement in campus activities as well as isolation from peers, staff, and faculty (Tatum, 1999).

Understanding a sense of belonging must be contextualized in regard to undocuBlack students.

Belonging and Race

It is no secret that the student demographics of higher education have evolved over the years, and college campuses are more diverse than ever. In 2021, more than 5.6 million students who were enrolled in higher education were from immigrant families (Batalova & Feldblum, 2023). Furthermore, a report by the American Immigration Council and the Presidents Alliance on Higher Education and Immigration (2023) noted that over 408,000 undocumented students were enrolled in higher education in 2021, representing 1.9% of all students enrolled that year. Within the undocumented student population, 45.7% identified as Hispanic, 27.2% as Asian, 13.8% as Black, and 10% identified as white. With increased diversity comes new experiences of belonging for different racial and ethnic groups on college campuses (Duran & Jones 2019). Scholars have studied belonging on college campuses for various racial and ethnic groups (see Freeman et al., 2007; Hausmann et al., 2007; Hurtado & Carter, 1997; Johnson et al., 2007; Museus & Maramba, 2011; Nunez, 2009; Strayhorn, 2019) and have found that students of color experience belonging differently than their white counterparts. For instance, students of color experience less sense of belonging on college campuses if they are in negative racial climates and if they have fewer interactions with faculty and peers (Hurtado & Carter, 1997; Johnson et al., 2007; Maramba & Velasquez, 2012). Furthermore, if students regard a campus as unwelcoming to their racial identity groups, they are less likely to feel as if they belong (Museus & Maramba, 2011; Nunez, 2009). However, Maramba and Velasquez (2012) illustrated that being connected to one's racial/ethnic group positively impacts belonging. Experiencing a strong sense of belonging is important for students of color because, as previously noted, belonging is linked to successful persistence in higher education.

Belonging and Engagement

Students also feel a sense of belonging on campus when they are engaged in activities or are involved in student organizations. Positive relationships with faculty and staff also increase students' sense of belonging, as illustrated by Hurtado's (2015) study; they found that support from faculty and staff helped students foster better relationships, which is critical to belonging. Based on the aforementioned studies, belonging is influenced by campus involvement as well as support from faculty and staff.

Belonging and Undocumented Students

While the literature on belonging and students of color is important, it is also imperative to understand how undocumented students experience belonging on college campuses. Not surprisingly, the literature on belonging for undocumented students mainly focuses on the Latinx population. There is very little literature on Black undocumented students' sense of belonging on college experiences; therefore, the positioning of belonging that I engage in focuses on Latinx undocumented students.

Browne and Odem (2012) contend that legal status is a strong predictor of belonging for undocumented students. Undocumented students can be deported from the country they believe to be their home (Abrego, 2006, 2008, 2018; Gonzales, 2011; Heeren, 2015). This lack of certainty affects their sense of belonging because they are navigating unknown circumstances that their peers are not experiencing. Belonging for undocumented students is difficult to obtain because they live at an intersection: the United States is their home, but their immigrant status does not recognize that (Torres-Olave et al., 2021; Negrón-González, 2014). Essentially, they live in a liminal space, one where they don't quite know where they belong to (Gonzales, 2011).

Undocumented students, specifically Latinx students, also experience social–emotional drain caused by their undocumented status (Ellis & Chen, 2013; Gámez et al., 2017). This emotional toll is a result of discrimination, fear of deportation, and other systemic barriers that limit success within higher education (Pérez, 2010).

As is true for all students, protective factors exist for undocumented students as well. For instance, having support from faculty, peers, and others is imperative for belonging for undocumented students (Hurtado et al., 2015; Strayhorn, 2019, 2020). According to Nunez (2009), when Latinx undocumented students are engaged in community and with their academics, they have a better sense of belonging.

As previously mentioned, the existing literature on belonging for undocumented students shares mostly one perspective: the Latinx position. Therefore, it does not include the variation of what belonging looks like for undocuBlack students, or undocuAsian students, or other groups with intersecting identities. It is important to note that while Latinx undocumented students face similar structural and legal barriers to higher education as undocuBlack immigrants, their experiences differ. Therefore, the current study is pivotal because it highlights how 15 undocuBlack immigrants experienced belonging throughout their collegiate experiences. While the 15 experiences referenced in this book are not an indication of how all undocuBlack students experience a sense of belonging, their experiences shed light on other undocumented experiences that should be considered.

Strayhorn's Framing

I center Strayhorn's (2012) definition to discuss the experiences of belonging for the undocuBlack participants within this study. According to Strayhorn (2012), a sense of belonging is created by a student's access to support on campus, connection, mattering, and feeling valued by a group. Essentially, students who experience a strong sense of belonging have opportunities to access resources, physical safe spaces, connection to faculty, staff, and administrators, and they feel valued by other students. These concepts of belonging have been corroborated by other studies as well (see Contreras, 2009; Gonzales et al., 2013; Hurtado et al., 2015; Teranishi et al., 2015). Using Strayhorn's definition, I suggest that belonging for the undocuBlack students within my study was affected by access to support on their respective campuses; connection to faculty, staff, and peers; and a belief that they mattered within their own student groups. The undocuBlack participants within the current study struggled to find resources to help them navigate financial difficulties and institutional policies; they experienced a lack of connection to peers, faculty, and staff; and if they had access to safe spaces, they felt othered and not valued by those groups.

Analysis of Belonging for UndocuBlack Students Within the Current Study

The 15 participants in the current study had varied experiences of belonging, and I center this discussion around their belonging in student spaces. Through those spaces, I consider their access to resources, connection to faculty and staff, and whether they felt they mattered to other students.

Of the 15 participants, 9 noted that they had access to undocumented student organizations on their campus, and only 4 had direct access to a USRC, otherwise known as DREAM Centers. Six of the nine joined the undocumented student organizations, but they each noted that they were the only Black person in the space. Additionally, they noted that the scholarships, the programming, the staffing, and the language in those groups were designed for and representative of the Latinx student population. The others who did not join undocumented spaces opted out because they feared being the only Black person in those groups; that fear stemmed from their ongoing experiences of not being recognized in spaces designated for undocumented students.

Additionally, of the 15 participants, there were 7 without DACA status; they noted that support for undocumented students on their campuses was intended for those with DACA status. Those without legal status were then alienated from staff, faculty, peers, and resources on their campuses.

Nine of the 15 participants joined Black Student Union (BSU), African Student Association (ASA), or other Caribbean-related organizations because they wanted to connect with other Black students. However, they noted that their time in those spaces did not validate their immigration status. Six participants did not join Black spaces because they felt that only the African American experience, and not the Black immigrant experience, would be validated.

Finally, five of the participants noted that they found belonging elsewhere, outside of campus. For instance, the UndocuBlack Network (UBN) provided a sense of support that faculty, staff, and other spaces on campus did not provide.

While all participants' experiences were unique, they all shared similar experiences related to belonging in spaces: they all struggled to feel a sense of belonging anywhere, and they believed that race played a factor in their lack of belonging on college campuses.

Lack of Belonging in Undocumented Spaces Within the Current Study

To get to the core of belonging, one of the questions I asked participants was, '*Did you join clubs or organizations on campus for undocumented students? If so, can you tell me more about this experience and whether race was a factor?*' At the heart of the question was the need for insight on whether college campuses had an adequate support for undocumented students.

There were two noteworthy categories of responses: (1) participants joined undocumented spaces because they had access to them, but they did not feel like they belonged because they were the only Black person in the space or because they did not have DACA status, and (2) participants did not have access to an undocumented space on their campus because they did not exist, which contributed to feeling a lack of belonging. I concluded that the undocuBlack participants experienced a lack of belonging because they did not have an adequate access to support services; they lacked the connection to faculty and staff because the individuals they interacted with did not represent the diversity of the undocumented population; and they felt othered from other undocumented students. Next, I share some of the responses to the aforementioned interview questions.

Category 1: Undocumented Students Who Had Access to and Were a Part of Undocumented Spaces

According to Taryn, a participant with DACA status,

> *I joined the DREAM Team because I was a Dream.US recipient. The club got disbanded because there was not enough funding. Race was a big factor in me joining because the only race we saw was Hispanic.[1] It was big, I'm going to be honest, it was a really big factor because one thing, especially with TheDream.US scholarship, I hate to say it, but the only race that we always saw were Hispanics. They would mainly speak Spanish so they would say something in English and then continue the conversation in Spanish. So that made it very difficult.*

At the time of the interview, Taryn had graduated from college. Because she was a recipient of TheDream.US scholarship, she was involved in the student club on campus for students who were awarded the scholarship. According to Taryn, while she was in TheDream.US space, she saw race as a factor that affected her experience. As noted by Taryn, the entire staff[2] was Latinx and would mainly speak in Spanish, which was a deterrent for her. Additionally, as the only Black student present, she did not feel that she could ask for support from staff as they were all representative of another culture. Even though Taryn had access to a space and support for undocumented students, her level of engagement was affected by the lack of diversity within the space. I concluded that she lacked a sense of belonging, even though she had access to an undocumented space that provided her with resources, because she did not feel connected to staff or students within that space.

According to Arion, a participant with DACA status,

> *I joined a club for DREAMers. Race was not a factor because if I knew I would be the only Black person, I would never join. In the DREAMers club, I am the only Black person and I always felt everyone was staring at me, and now when I see people on campus, they act like they don't remember me.*

At the time of the interview, Arion was in his final year of his undergraduate education at a private institution in California. He also had a full scholarship and an internship on campus and lived within four miles from his college campus. Arion did join the undocumented space on his campus, but he was the only Black person present. As he noted, he was unable to consider race because if he did, it would have stopped him from joining the space. While he still joined despite his own fear of being the only Black person, he never felt comfortable in that space because of his race. Additionally, because Arion was at a private school, he was a standout in the group because it was a smaller campus. As a result of being the only Black person in the space, Arion never felt like he belonged in the undocumented space because of lack of connection to peers, faculty, and staff.

According to Greg, a participant with DACA status,

I was in the DREAM Center. . . . I did not participate too much, but I did participate in some of the events, and it was a good place for me to just kind of get extra resources on how to navigate my problems. I think race played a factor. Sometimes people would be surprised because everybody in those clubs are usually Latino and you know, I was like one of the only like Black people in the club or whatever, but people were very welcoming about it.

At the time of the interview, Greg had recently concluded his undergraduate experience and was working at a startup in San Francisco. Greg had access to a DREAM Center on his campus and noted that the space was useful for him to access resources and discuss his difficulties with being undocumented. Within the space, Greg felt fairly comfortable because the members were accepting. However, he mentioned that the space lacked diversity, but he did not let that stop him from being engaged with the student organization. While he was engaged and had access to resources, two of the factors Strayhorn notes as related to belonging, he never felt a sense of belonging with the group; he saw them more as a resource hub.

According to Shannon, a participant without DACA status,

I participated in a student-led undocumented fund and organization. I was the only Black student in that club. I was fortunate, because the people around me were very welcoming. But, not having DACA made me feel isolated. With ally-training, I would get asked to speak for Black voices.

At the time of the interview, Shannon had recently graduated from college. She reflected on her collegiate experience and her access to an undocumented student space. For Shannon, while she had access to a space, her lack of belonging stemmed from not having DACA status. As noted by Shannon, as a result of her unDACAmented status, she did not feel connected within the group. She also discussed the burden of being the only Black person within the space because it led to her having to serve as the expert on issues related to the undocuBlack experience. Ultimately, Shannon had access to a space that provided her with resources and a welcoming community. However, her disconnect happened because of a lack of diversity within the space.

According to Anthony, a participant without DACA status,

> *I was talking about the DREAM Center. I was the only Black person there, but other than that, race was not a factor for me. I go to the DREAM Center and they have little events. There's mostly Hispanics there and there are not a lot of Black people, Africans there, so that's like the only thing. I cannot believe I'm the only Black or African American undocumented student in the school.*

At the time of the interview, Anthony was in his second year at a community college in California. He had access to a DREAM Center and joined the space in hopes of accessing resources and community. It is also imperative to note that Anthony did not attend high school in the United States. For Anthony, race was not a factor in joining the undocumented space. However, he did note that he was always shocked that he was the only Black student in the space, but he continued to utilize the resources. He wanted to have access to resources, which the center provided him with. I concluded that while Anthony did not see race as a limiting factor to the undocumented space, he did not feel a sense of belonging because of his own identities and position within those spaces.

Summary

Taryn, Arion, Greg, Shannon, and Anthony all had access to an undocumented student space on their campuses. While they joined, they still felt a lack of belonging because staff and students within those centers were not reflective of the diversity of the undocumented population. However, the five participants did note that they had access to resources through those centers or groups, which helped them as they navigated higher education.

Category 2: Undocumented Students Who Had Access to But Were Not a Part of Undocumented Spaces

According to Gabby, a participant without DACA status,

> *I did not join any because I did not want to be the only Black student. If they had a group, I would only join if it was for Black undocumented students.*

Race would've played a factor; I feel like as a Black undocumented person, my struggles are different from a Hispanic undocumented person. We go through racial issues here and because we're undocumented, we go through issues that they don't necessarily go through, so I feel like our struggles are different.

At the time of the interview, Gabby had already graduated from the college and was currently in law school in Florida. During her undergraduate studies, Gabby had access to an undocumented student space on her campus but opted not to join the space because she felt uncomfortable as a Black immigrant. According to Gabby, she knew first hand that her undocumented experience was different from her Hispanic peers, and she did not feel that the space would acknowledge those intersections. Additionally, Gabby noted the stressors she experienced as an undocuBlack person and believed an organization for undocumented students would need to consider those additional factors. As a result of not being involved with the undocumented space, Gabby did not feel a sense of belonging on her campus.

According to Fatima, a participant with DACA status,

There was a DACA org. It was a great club, but I did not get involved with it. I was more focused on my career trajectory and how I was going to use this opportunity to my advantage. All clubs were tailored to my career. I rarely joined any social clubs. I joined college democrats. I think race was a factor seeing that all the students in the DACA clubs were of Hispanic background and I don't really identify with them.

When I interviewed Fatima, she was in her final year of her undergraduate education at an HBCU on a full academic scholarship from TheDream.US. As noted by Fatima, she did have an access to a space for undocumented students, but she did not participate. Fatima wanted to be in spaces that catered to her professional journey, and she did not see the benefits in joining the undocumented student space on her campus. However, she was heavily involved on campus with internships and other student organizations. Fatima's experience of belonging was unique because while she did not feel connected to faculty, staff, and peers from the undocumented student group, she felt connected through other organizations. She also had an access to resources that contributed to her feeling like she belonged on campus. It is important to note that while she felt a sense of belonging as a result of other factors, she did not gain that from the undocumented spaces. Therefore, I conclude that Fatima did not feel like she belonged within undocumented spaces because she did not join a space for undocumented students out of fear that her experiences would not be validated.

According to Raven, a participant without DACA status,

I don't feel comfortable in those spaces. I think there's a lot more support for Hispanic/Latinx undocumented/DACAmented students. I think that is a bit close-minded of me, but I just never thought I had much in common with those students so I never thought to join clubs/organizations for undocumented students.

At the time of the interview, Raven was in her second year as an undergraduate student. Raven noted that as a Black immigrant and someone without DACA status, she did not feel that she would have anything in common with other undocumented students. Her barriers to connection were a result of her immigration status and her race. Participants like Raven were unique in that not only did race isolate them from their peers but so did DACA status. I concluded that Raven did not feel a sense of belonging because she lacked access to staff, faculty, peers, and resources. Additionally, while she had access to space for undocumented students, she thought she would be 'othered' which also limited her access to the space. Finally, without DACA status, she was further isolated from the community.

Summary

Fatima had access to an undocumented student space on her campus but did not join out of fear of being 'othered'. Raven and Gabby also had access to an undocumented space but struggled to belong because they did not have DACA. Without DACA, they felt isolated from their community, and the events, resources, and programming were tailored to the Latinx-DACAmented students. Ultimately, while they all had varied experiences, I concluded that they did not feel a sense of belonging because they did not connect with faculty, staff, and peers, even though they had access to a space and resources.

Category 3: Undocumented Students Without Access to Undocumented Spaces

According to Rosemary, a participant without DACA status,

I did not join any clubs for undocumented students because they did not exist. If they existed, maybe I would've joined. I just haven't always felt comfortable with this identity, so I wouldn't have felt comfortable being in a space to discuss it like that. Also, a lot of times when people would refer me to different pages or like websites and scholarships, they would mostly, 95% be tailored towards the Latinx Community. So, I feel like there isn't that much support for Black undocumented people. I don't think race would've been a roadblock for me, but I think DACA vs. non-DACA would've been what stopped me from joining.

At the time of the interview, Rosemary had recently graduated college and was applying to PhD programs. She described her undergraduate experience through the lens of someone without access to DACA. For Rosemary, even if she wanted to join a space for undocumented students, she could not because they did not exist on her campus. Rosemary was also unsure if she would have joined if one existed because of her fear that the resources would have been catered to the Latinx students and that her Blackness would have 'othered' her. In summation, Rosemary did not experience a sense of belonging because of her further pronounced immigrant status and being an undocuBlack person. Ultimately, she did not have access to resources, community, or space.

According to Lucy, the only participant in the study with TPS status,

Yeah, so I was not aware of any undocumented organizations that were at my undergrad institution. And I will also say that I had to work two jobs and I was volunteering in a research lab for my CV so it just didn't leave a lot of time for extracurriculars and I had the UndocuBlack Network.

At the time of the interview, she was in her first year of her PhD program. As an undergraduate student, Lucy did not have access to an undocumented student space on her campus. However, she also worked multiple jobs and did not have time to participate in activities on campus. Additionally, she had connections to the UndocuBlack Network which provided her with the community she wanted. For Lucy, her belonging on campus was altered because she had other duties that made it hard for her to engage on campus. I concluded that while she lacked belonging on her campus because of lack of access to resources, space, and community, she created a sense of belonging through the UndocuBlack Network.

According to Abraham, a participant without access to DACA

I joined a strong community when I found out about the UndocuBlack Network, not from school, it was a national organization. I definitely have felt more of a community in UndocuBlack. . . . Race played a factor in me joining UndocuBlack because we have a lot of folks in the Caribbean, as you definitely know. I thought I would feel more connected for sure, and you definitely feel visible in the struggle.

At the time of the interview, Abraham had already graduated with his bachelor's and master's degrees. He recounted both of his experiences, but the quote above is only reflective of his undergraduate experience. Abraham did not have access to a space for undocumented students when he was an undergraduate student, but he did have a connection with the UndocuBlack Network. For Abraham, the UndocuBlack Network provided him with a safe space to belong because there were other Black people within the space, who understood his experience as a undocuBlack student. In summation, Abraham lacked belonging on his campus as a result of lack of access to resources, safe spaces, and community with faculty, staff, and peers. However, he found his community and sense of belonging outside of the college campus environment.

The following four participants did not expound on their lack of access to an undocumented student space nor if race played a factor.

According to Teresa, a participant with DACA status,

No, we don't have anything on this campus.

Darius, a participant with DACA status, said:

I looked into clubs, but I did not find any.

Mitch, a participant without DACA status, said:

They don't have any clubs for undocumented students on campus.

Sasha, a participant without DACA, said:

I did not join any because they don't exist.

Summary

Rosemary, Lucy, Abraham, Teresa, Sasha, Darius, Mitch, and Sasha did not have access to an undocumented student space on their campuses. Without access to a space, these students did not have a place they could belong to and connect with others who shared a similar immigration status. According to Torres-Olave et al. (2021), undocumented students need to experience belonging in spaces on campus because it gives them a sense of membership and intimacy. It is important for undocumented students to have access to spaces of belonging. Yet, the undocuBlack participants in the current study struggled to connect with staff and students in undocumented spaces. They did not see staff in those centers who were Black. This lack of representation affected the way they interacted with those spaces designed for them to feel safe. They wanted to interact with staff in those spaces, who understood their experiences, but they did not have that opportunity; while some of the staff present in those spaces shared their undocumented identity, they did not have experience with the intersection of race.

For undocuBlack participants in the study who did not have access to a DREAM Center or a USRC, they also experienced a lack of belonging. This lack of belonging motivated them not to be engaged in campus activities. They were further isolated from the campus environment. In undocumented spaces, they had no connection with others because of race. The students in the current study struggled to feel a sense of belonging anywhere.

Lack of Belonging in Black Spaces Within the Current Study

Another important highlight from the current study is that while undocuBlack students felt they did not belong in undocumented spaces, they had similar feelings in Black student spaces as well. While this finding was not surprising because Black Americans have experiences different from undocuBlack people, it is important to contextualize the undocuBlack participants' experiences in these spaces as well. UndocuBlack participants within the current study noted that they experienced a silencing of their undocumented identity whenever they occupied Black student spaces; whenever they were present in Black spaces, their immigrant status was never mentioned or celebrated. However, participants were adamant that while their race was the first identity that others noticed, their immigrant status placed more boundaries on their existence. So, the lack of belonging they experienced in Black spaces was not as impactful on their experiences as an undocumented person, yet still necessary to discuss.[3]

Of the 15 undocuBlack immigrants in the study, 9 of them joined a Black Student Union (BSU), African Student Association (ASA), or other Caribbean-related organizations because they wanted to connect with other Black students. Six participants never joined Black spaces. However, the students who did join Black spaces felt that their time in those spaces did not validate their immigration status or their Blackness. Through the questions '*Did you join any clubs on campus for Black students? What was that experience like?*', I was able to understand their experiences in those spaces. One of the main reasons I asked that question was to understand how their Black identity affected their sense of belonging on campus with other Black students. It was clear through their responses and my analyses that they joined Black spaces for a sense of connection to their community but instead experienced a silencing of their immigration status and isolation from the Black community.

Category One: Participants Who Joined Black Student Spaces on Campus

Arion, a participant from Jamaica, said,

> *I am in the Black student union but never really go to any of their meetings. I just feel like I am not African American, so I felt distant between Black Americans. I want to go, but no immigration status was ever mentioned.*

Arion joined the BSU to gain connection to his peers but instead felt distanced because he never knew if his immigration status would be recognized. I concluded that Arion did not feel like he belonged in the BSU on his campus because his immigration status isolated him from the group.

Taryn, a participant from Barbados, said,

> *I minored in African and Caribbean studies so I joined all those clubs. Immigration was not brought up, it was laughed about. We would change the subject.*

Taryn was involved in many Black student organizations on her campus as a result of her major. However, she noted that an undocumented immigrant status would be considered a joke in those spaces. In Taryn's case, while undocumented status was considered, it was mocked from a place of misunderstanding. In summation, Taryn did not feel connected to her Black peers, nor did she find a safe place in the Black student spaces.

Rosemary, a participant from Jamaica, said,

> *So I joined a Caribbean student association and the Black student Union. Immigration was only mentioned in terms of discussing differences between like first generation immigrants. So my experience is I'm an observant and I pay attention to the differences between different types of people. With BSU, I felt like it was mostly African Americans, and I feel like I could never relate to African Americans completely either.*

As for Rosemary, she did join a Caribbean student club and BSU. She noted that first-generation immigrants would be discussed but nothing related to immigrant status. Additionally, she noted that she never really connected to the African American experience within the BSU on her campus. Again, Rosemary did not feel that she belonged in Black spaces because of the lack of community and connection to her Black peers.

Greg, a participant from Togo, said,

I was a general member in BSU. I had a leadership role for the national society of Black engineers and I also had a leadership role for the African student association at the university as well. So, BSU I didn't find that productive with my time, but the National Society of Black Engineers was definitely like a good place for me. I think that was very productive, as well as the African student association. I think with the BSU they kind of like more focused on pop culture, instead of history. As far as was immigration was ever mentioned. In ASA, some of the students were international students, so in that regard, it was mentioned, but not in the you know, being an international student and being undocumented are very different.

Greg was involved in multiple student organizations focused on Black students, and he had different experiences within them. Greg was not an active participant in BSU, but he joined in hopes of connection to his peers. He did not find BSU particularly helpful for his sense of belonging. As for ASA, he noted there were other immigrant students, so that provided him with a sense of connection to his peers. Finally, in the Black engineers group, he felt connected because of the academic topic area. It can be concluded that Greg's identities had to operate in a silo for him to fit in or connect with his peers.

Darius, a participant from Trinidad, said,

I was part of SOCA, which is a Caribbean organization as well as Black Student Union. My experience was that I never told anyone I was undocumented, just blended and flowed and did all the things. Everyone knew I was from Trinidad and I grew up there, but no one ever questioned why I did not go back for spring break. Immigration was never mentioned.

Darius was another participant who joined two Black student organizations to seek community. Darius took a different approach from his peers because he joined a SOCA club, which centered his Trinidadian experience, and he also joined a BSU. In the BSU, he felt less isolated because he had community elsewhere. Additionally, he never discussed his immigration status with students in the BSU and decided to just blend in with the community. I concluded that Darius lacked belonging because he could never truly exist as an undocuBlack student.

Abraham, a participant from Senegal, said,

It's multifaceted when you're undocumented and Black, so in those clubs, I just connected with the Africans in those clubs about being in the U.S. Yeah, so I'll say in those two spaces, I mainly focus on my African identity, so I am Black in America, but undocumented. It was more focused on my Blackness and Africanness, but never my undocumented status.

Abraham joined two organizations in hopes that his experience in them could honor his multilayered identities. In one space, his African culture was celebrated which provided him with a sense of belonging. In the BSU space, his blackness was recognized, but his immigrant identity was dormant. Ultimately, he could never really exist in one space with all of his intersecting identities but found ways to connect with Black students in different ways. I conclude that because he had to separate his identities, he felt he did not belong in any space.

Faith, a participant from Nigeria, said,

I joined the African Students Association Club during my freshman and sophomore years, but I don't think it was specific to Black people. I did not attend enough of their events to know if immigration was ever mentioned, but I think since they were all immigrants, I assume it would've been mentioned.

While Faith joined a student organization for African students, she rarely engaged with them. As a follow-up to Faith's response, I did ask her why she did not participate, and she noted that she wanted to focus on other types of connection on campus.

Teresa, a participant from Malawi, said,

Yes, I'm a part of Black Students United and actually this semester, I did a presentation called same race, different culture where I presented topics that are within Black culture and the first one that I did was that immigration is a Black issue, so I talked about DACA. We talk about immigration status. It's been very interesting because a lot of people didn't know, a lot of people thought that being undocumented or having DACA had to do with being Mexican. A lot of people were shocked.

Teresa's experience was different from most of the participants in the study because she decided to be the one to educate the students in Black spaces. She noted that the students were shocked once they learned that immigration was also a 'Black issue' which demonstrates the lack of knowledge that the Black community has regarding immigration. Fortunately, for Teresa, because she took on the role of an educator, she did not feel isolated within the Black space that she occupied on campus. She felt a sense of belonging through being an educator.

Shannon, a participant from Kenya, said,

I was part of BSU and Nigerian Student Association (NSA), but status was never mentioned in those clubs. Both organizations did a collaborative event. . . . Also, I was in the East African Student Association, and I stayed more involved with the African clubs.

Shannon joined multiple clubs on campus for Black students. She wanted to relate to her peers and share similar experiences. Unfortunately, she had to join numerous clubs to feel a connection to Black students. Each club had their own mission. She related more to the African student clubs because her African culture was celebrated. Therefore, Shannon found belonging in African spaces but not Black American spaces.

Summary

Another important aspect of sense of belonging for students on college campuses is peer-to-peer connection. Furthermore, students with intersecting identities aim to find community and connection with other students (Valdez & Golash-Boza, 2020). Student connection is important for persistence within higher education, and the undocuBlack participants in the current study did not have strong connections with other students, which further impacted their sense of belonging. The undocuBlack participants in the current study did not have a struggle on whether they should join a Black student space. Unlike their internal struggle about whether to join an undocumented space, they eagerly wanted to join a Black space for connection and community to their peers. However, the participants who joined BSUs described their experience as not being recognized as immigrants but being categorized as African American, which made belonging in those spaces difficult. The undocuBlack participants in the study also found other avenues for belonging in African and Caribbean student spaces on campus. Nonetheless, while participants in the current study found ways to connect to Black students, they ultimately did not feel they belonged in Black American spaces because of their intersections as undocuBlack immigrants. They were never recognized as Black, undocumented, and immigrant; they had to exist as one in certain spaces.

Category Two: Participants Who Did Not Join Any Black Student Spaces

Sasha, a participant from Trinidad, said,

I haven't joined. . . . I have a unique Black experience, and I have a difficult time when I get into spaces, and first of all, there's people who believe that people from Africa and the Caribbean aren't Black. So, I have a difficult time being in those spaces because I don't consider myself African American. I consider myself Black. And you know, to be Black does not mean that you're African American, but to be African American does mean that you're Black, and I think that a lot of people miss that, so I just have a really difficult time navigating a lot of those spaces.

Sasha never felt that she connected with the African American culture within Black student organizations. Sasha opted to not join Black spaces on her campus out of fear that the culture would solely be centered around the African American experience. She had no sense of belonging with Black students on her campus.

Raven, a participant from Jamaica, said,

Yes. I find it difficult to connect with African American students, because I'm Caribbean and Black. So I often find that there's not many similarities between our cultures for us to bond with, and I even find it difficult connecting with Caribbean people who are born in the US versus those who are born in Jamaica.

Raven felt there were distinct differences with African Americans, Caribbeans who were raised in their origin country, and Caribbeans who were raised in America. As a result of this, she decided to not join any student organizations on her campus that were focused on uplifting Black students because she assumed her culture would be disregarded. She had no sense of belonging with the Black community on her campus.

Anthony, a participant from Imo State, said,

No, I did not join any because basically my days look like I am either working a lot or trying to focus on school and it's a lot of catching up. So either I try to focus on school, then I would be struggling financially.

Anthony's experience with not joining was related to his hectic schedule. For Anthony, he could not join any student organizations because he did not have time, so he decided to focus on school. It is important to note that Anthony did join the DREAM Center on his campus because he wanted access to resources. Anthony felt he could forego his connection to Black student spaces because of that reason. In summation, Anthony did not get a chance to experience a sense of belonging within Black student spaces.

Gabby, a participant from Kenya, said,

I didn't join any specifically for Black students in undergrad, but right now I'm in Black Law Students Association in law school. I love the experience, it's like all the Black people in the school getting together. We don't talk about immigration, we discuss Black issues. People don't know that Black people go through this like when you think I'm undocumented person you don't think Black, you think Hispanic.

Gabby did not join any Black spaces in her undergraduate experience.

Lucy, a participant from Haiti, said,

There was a Black Student Union that I could've joined, but I felt that I had a large support system with the UndocuBlack Network and I was just working all of the time. So I felt like I just did not have the time to pursue that. Especially because within UndocuBlack Network, I met so many amazing people, and I have so many friends. And a lot of us are going to college, even if it's in other states, and so I felt like I had a personal support group and I just didn't need to pursue that in school or be disappointed if I tried to pursue it and it just wasn't there.

Lucy's experience was unique in that she felt she already had community through the UndocuBlack Network so she did not seek to join Black student spaces on her campus. While she did not gain a sense of belonging on campus through Black student organizations, she had it elsewhere.

Mitch, a participant from Gabon, said,

No, I did not join. I was in the multicultural club and part of undocuBlack. I just think it [immigration status] would not be mentioned.

Mitch opted to not join Black spaces out of fear he would not be recognized.

Summary

As mentioned earlier, access to physical safe spaces on college campuses is important to the sense of belonging for undocumented students. According to Gonzales (2016), once undocumented students enroll in higher education, they are often met with intolerable campus environments, which contribute to feelings of being an outsider. Additionally, according to Solórzano et al. (2000), Black students often create counter spaces to experience belonging. Within the current study, the undocuBlack participants had varied experiences with Black student spaces on college campuses. The ones who joined mostly did so for connection to community, and the ones who did not join opted out because of fear that their immigrant identity would not be recognized; they had busy work schedules; or they had community elsewhere. However, the ones who did join Black spaces felt like they did not belong. Therefore, the undocuBlack students in this study had an incessant battle with where they belonged. One space provided them with a sense of 'in-group', and the other provided them with 'resources'. In Black spaces, while they could not fully exist as an undocumented immigrant, they could engage in their Blackness. As a result, the undocuBlack immigrants in this study were constantly compartmentalizing their experiences so they could belong in spaces designated for them.

Finding Belonging Elsewhere: The UndocuBlack Network

While some undocuBlack students from the current study did not feel like they belonged anywhere on their campus, some of them found refuge in outside spaces like the UndocuBlack Network. The UndocuBlack Network is an organization that works to bridge the gap between undocumented and formerly undocumented people. They aim for racial justice for Black undocumented people. Among the 15 undocuBlack immigrants in the current study, 5 of them noted that they were members of the UndocuBlack Network and that the network had a positive influence on their collegiate experience and sense of belonging. When asked how they found out about the UndocuBlack Network, they all noted that they had a high school teacher or college counselor who introduced them to the organization. The quotes given next provide further context.

Abraham said,

I joined a strong community when I found out about the UndocuBlack Network, a national organization. There were a lot of folks from the Caribbean, as you definitely know. I felt more connected for sure, and you definitely feel visible in the struggle.

For Abraham, the UndocuBlack Network was a safe place where he could connect with others who shared similar experiences. Abraham was one of the participants who did not have access to undocumented spaces on his campus, so the UndocuBlack Network provided him with a sense of belonging. Abraham was introduced to this network through a teacher, which shows the necessity of representation for undocumented students.

Lucy said,

Within UndocuBlack Network, I met so many amazing people, and I have so many friends and a lot of us are going to college, even if it's in other states, and so I felt like I had a personal support group and I just didn't need to pursue that in school or be disappointed if I tried to pursue it and it just wasn't there. During my senior year of high school, I was introduced to this by one teacher, she was amazing and I learned about UndocuBlack through her, because in my senior year I decided to come out and just to let everybody know, disclose that I wasn't documented and so I learned through her.

Similar to Abraham, Lucy wanted a space where she belonged. While Lucy had access to a BSU on her campus, she never joined because she believed the space would not be all encompassing of her experiences as an undocuBlack student. The UndocuBlack Network provided her with a sense of community and connection to others. She was also introduced to the UndocuBlack Network through a teacher.

Mitch said,

I had one teacher who was part of the UndocuBlack Network; she was from Trinidad, and she helped me go to college and get scholarships. She was my favorite teacher, so I joined the UndocuBlack Network because of all the similarities.

Mitch was also another participant who expressed his appreciation for the UndocuBlack Network as a space that provided him with somewhere to belong. Similar to Abraham and Lucy, Mitch was introduced to the UndocuBlack Network through a teacher.

Gabby said,

I went to the undocuBlack convening in Philly, and it was amazing because we went out, and everybody had their passports. And I was like oh my God, I don't feel lonely, like I'm not the only one that's pulling out my passport. So I loved being in the same room as every single person, because you just knew, like every single person was either once undocumented or they currently are undocumented.

Gabby noted that her experience with the UndocuBlack Network gave her a space to be with others who had shared experiences.

Summary

While not all participants mentioned the UndocuBlack Network as a community they joined, it was clear that they all yearned to belong to a space like the UndocuBlack Network. Unfortunately, not all participants were exposed to the network. Furthermore, the collaboration with spaces like the UndocuBlack Network should be highlighted; I discuss this further in Chapter 8.

It is paramount that practitioners, scholars, and administrators realize that creating spaces like the UndocuBlack Network on campuses is important for student persistence, especially for vulnerable groups like undocuBlack students. Prior literature has noted that undocumented students frequently interact with staff who are not informed about immigration policies, which leads to further disengagement and lack of belonging for undocumented students (Contreras, 2009; Nienhusser et al., 2016; Nienhusser, 2018). Therefore, this demonstrates the need for undocuBlack students to have competent staff who understand their experiences. Colleges and universities should invest in faculty and staff who are undocu-competent (Nienhusser & Espino, 2016; Tapia-Fuselier, 2019, 2021; Valenzuela et al., 2015). Undocu-competence refers to practitioners who can advocate for undocumented students and understand their unique experiences (Tapia-Fuselier, 2021, 2022). 'Therefore, it is crucial that colleges and universities provide undocuBlack students with access to faculty and staff members who are informed about immigration and the issues facing the undocumented students they serve' (Russell, 2022). Other scholars note that positive interactions with students and faculty lead to success in higher education (Contreras, 2009; Perez & Rodriguez, 2011; Perez, 2010, 2011). Conversely, without a connection to faculty, staff, and peers, students experience a lack of belonging.

Further Implications: Where Do We Go From Here?

The 15 participants in this study were all successfully persisting or had persisted despite the lack of belonging they experience within higher education. However, the undocuBlack participants felt a lack of connection to their peers, faculty, and staff; invalidated in Black and undocumented spaces; and did not feel like they mattered. It is my hope that the discussion above provides an opportunity for inquiry into the collegiate experiences of undocuBlack students from scholars, educators, practitioners, policymakers, and even students.

Scholars should further investigate the experiences of undocuBlack students, whether related to Black cultural centers' role in providing a sense of belonging for undocuBlack immigrant students or the evaluation of programming and support structures in DREAM Centers. Additionally, the findings on the lack of belonging should elicit questions on the important role that race plays in impacting the undocumented student experience. Scholars should also critique the homogeneity of the research that extensively centers the experiences of Latinx undocumented students and seek to include and challenge systems of oppression and privilege to make the experiences of undocuBlack students and the inequities of the legal and institutional policies visible. Finally, further research is needed on current organizations working to support and uplift the Black immigrant experience (I will shed light on a few organizations in the final chapter).

Practitioners and educators should challenge the current foundations of learning about the undocumented community to include the diverse experiences of Black undocumented students. Furthermore, this study should inform practices on how to center the experiences of undocuBlack students in the classroom or through programming.

Students should invite those who might be 'othered', especially in undocumented and Black spaces.

Policymakers should engage with immigration policies and immigration, enforcement, and customs policies, asking questions about who is disproportionately impacted by the laws.

Once we understand the experiences of undocuBlack students, we can create more inclusive higher education policies and challenge immigration policies that aim to further marginalize people of color. This study informs us on how we can center the voices of undocuBlack students without decentering others. The final chapter digs deeper into this concept.[4]

Notes

1. Hispanic is an ethnicity, not a race, but wanted to keep the quote as it is from the participant.
2. It is important to note that Taryn had graduated in 2019. Since that time, The-Dream.US staff has expanded.
3. My next research project will explore the experiences of undocuBlack immigrants in Black cultural centers on college campuses.
4. To understand more about the undocuBlack participants' experiences specifically with faculty and staff, please refer to my dissertation: The Invisibility of UndocuBlack Students Within the Undocumented Community in Higher Education. I expand on those experiences in the dissertation.

References

Abrego, L. (2006). "I can't go to college because I don't have papers": Incorporation patterns of Latino undocumented youth. *Latino Studies, 4*(3), 212–231. https://doi.org/10.1057/palgrave.lst.8600200

Abrego, L. (2008). Legitimacy, social identity, and the mobilization of law: The effects of assembly bill 540 on undocumented students in California. *Law & Social Inquiry, 33*(3), 709–734. https://doi.org/10.1111/j.1747-4469.2008.00119.

Abrego, L. (2018). Renewed optimism and spatial mobility: Legal consciousness of Latino deferred action for childhood arrivals recipients and their families in Los Angeles. *Ethnicities, 18*(2), 192–207. https://doi.org/10.1177/1468796817752563

American Immigration Council and Presidents' Alliance on Higher Education and Immigration. (2023). (rep.). *Undocumented students in higher education how many students are in U.S. colleges and universities, and who are they?* Retrieved from www.higheredimmigrationportal.org/research/undocumented-students-in-higher-education-updated-march-2021/.

Batalova, J., & Feldblum, M. (2023). (rep.). *Investing in the future: Higher Ed should give greater focus to growing immigrant-origin student population.*

Migration Policy Institute and Presidents Alliance on Higher Education & Immigration. Retrieved from www.higheredimmigrationportal.org/research/immigrant-origin-students-in-u-s-higher-education/.

Browne, I., & Odem, M. (2012). "Juan Crow" in the Nuevo South?: Racialization of Guatemalan and Dominican immigrants in the Atlanta metro area. *Du Bois Review: Social Science Research on Race, 9*(2), 321–337. https://doi.org/10.1017/S1742058X1200015X

Contreras, F. (2009). Sin papeles y rompiendo barreras: Latino students and the challenges of persisting in college. *Harvard Educational Review, 79,* 610–632.

Duran, A., & Jones, S. R. (2019). Using intersectionality in qualitative research on college student identity development: Considerations, tensions, and possibilities. *Journal of College Student Development, 60*(4), 455–471. https://doi.org/10.1353/csd.2019.0040

Ellis, L. M., & Chen, E. C. (2013). Negotiating identity development among undocumented immigrant college students: A grounded theory study. *Journal of Counseling Psychology, 60,* 251–264. https://doi.org/10.1037/a0031350

Freeman, T. M., Anderman, L. H., & Jensen, J. M. (2007). Sense of belonging in college freshmen at the classroom and campus levels. *Journal of Experimental Education, 75,* 203–220. https://doi.org/10.3200/JEXE.75.3.203-220

Gámez, R., Lopez, W., & Overton, B. (2017). Mentors, resiliency, and ganas: Factors influencing the success of DACAmented, undocumented, and immigrant students in higher education. *Journal of Hispanic Higher Education, 16,* 144–161. https://doi.org/10.1177/1538192717697755

Gonzales, R. G. (2011). Learning to be illegal: Undocumented youth and shifting legal contexts in the transition to adulthood. *American Sociological Review, 76,* 602–619.

Gonzales, R. G. (2016). *Lives in limbo: Undocumented and coming of age in America.* University of California Press.

Gonzales, R. G., Suárez-Orozco, C., & Dedios-Sanguineti, M. C. (2013). No place to belong: Contextualizing concepts of mental health among undocumented immigrant youth in the United States. *American Behavioral Scientist, 57,* 1174–1199. https://doi.org/10.1177/0002764213487349

Hausmann, L., Schofield, J., & Woods, R. (2007). Sense of belonging as a predictor of intentions to persist among African American and White first-year college students. *Research in Higher Education, 48*(7), 803–839. https://doi.org/10.1007/s11162-007-9052-9

Heeren, G. (2015). The status of nonstatus. *The American University Law Review, 64,* 1115–1182.

Hurtado, S., Alvarado, A. R., & Guillermo-Wann, C. (2015). Creating inclusive environments: The mediating effects of faculty and staff validation on the relationship of discrimination/bias to students' sense of belonging. *Journal Committed to Social Change on Race and Ethnicity, 1,* 60–81.

Hurtado, S., & Carter, F. (1997). Effects of college transition and perceptions of the campus racial climate on Latino college students' sense of belonging. *Sociology of Education, 70*(4), 324–345. https://doi.org/10.2307/2673270.

Johnson, D. R., Soldner, M., Leonard, J. B., Alvarez, P., Inkelas, K. K., Rowan-Kenyon, H. T., . . . Longerbeam, S. D. (2007). Examining sense of belonging among first-year undergraduates from different racial/ethnic groups. *Journal of College Student Development, 48*(5), 525–542. https://doi.org/10.1353/csd.2007.0054.

Maramba, D. C., & Velasquez, P. (2012). Influences of the campus experience on the ethnic identity development of students of color. *Education and Urban Society, 44*(3), 294–317. https://doi.org/10.1177/0013124510393239.

Museus, S. D., & Maramba, D. C. (2011). The impact of culture on Filipino American students' sense of belonging. *Review of Higher Education, 34*, 231–258. https://doi.org/10.1353/rhe.2010.0022

Negrón-González, G. (2014). Undocumented youth activism as counter-spectacle: Civil disobedience and testimonio in the battle around immigration reform. *Aztlán, 40,* 87–112.

Nienhusser, H. (2018). Higher education institutional agents as policy implementers: The case of policies that affect undocumented and DACAmented students. *The Review of Higher Education, 41*(3), 423–453. https://doi.org/10.1353/rhe.2018.0014

Nienhusser, H. K., & Espino, M. M. (2016). Incorporating undocumented/DACAmented status competency into higher education institutional agents' practice. *Journal of Student Affairs Research and Practice, 54*(1), 1–14 https://doi.org/10.1080/19496591.2016.1194286

Nienhusser, K., Vega, B., & Carquin, M. (2016). Undocumented students' experiences with microaggressions during their college choice process. *Teachers College, 118*(2), 1–33.

Nunez, A. (2009). A critical paradox? Predictors of Latino students' sense of belonging in college. *Journal of Diversity in Higher Education, 2*(1), 46–61. https://doi.org/10.1037/a0014099

Pérez, P. A., & Rodriguez, J. L. (2011). Access and opportunity for Latina/o undocumented college students: Familial and institutional support factors. *Journal of the Association of Mexican American Educators, 5*(1), 14–21.

Pérez, W. (2010). Higher education access for undocumented students: Recommendations for counseling professionals. *Journal of College Admission, 206,* 32–35.

Pérez, W. (2011). *Americans by heart: Undocumented Latino students and the promise of higher education.* Teachers College Press.

Russell, F. (2022). *The invisibility of undocuBlack students within the undocumented community in higher education* [Doctoral dissertation, Temple University]. Theses and Dissertations. https://doi.org/10.34944/dspace/7734

Solorzano, D., Ceja, M., & Yosso, T. (2000). Critical race theory, racial microaggressions, and campus racial climate: The experiences of African American college students. *The Journal of Negro Education, 69*(1/2), 60–73. Retrieved from www.jstor.org/stable/2696265

Strayhorn, T. L. (2012). *College students' sense of belonging: A key to educational success.* Routledge.

Strayhorn, T. L. (2019). *College students' sense of belonging: A key to educational success for all students* (2nd ed.). Routledge.

Strayhorn, T. L. (2020). Measuring the relation between sense of belonging, campus leadership, and academic achievement for African American students at Historically Black Colleges and Universities (HBCUs): A "gender equity" analysis. *Journal of Minority Achievement, Creativity, and Leadership, 1*(1), 94–118. https://doi.org/10.5325/minoachicrealead.1.1.0094

Tapia-Fuselier, N. (2019). Undocumented students, community colleges, and the urgent call for undocu-competence. *Journal of Student Affairs, 28,* 145–152.

Tapia-Fuselier, N. (2021). Enhancing institutional undocu-competence through establishing undocumented student resource centers: A student-encompassed approach. *Journal of College Access, 6*(2), 132–145.

Tapia-Fuselier, N. (2022). "We do it all": Understanding the experiences of undocumented student resource center professionals. *Innovative Higher Education, 48*(3), 457–475. https://doi.org/10.1007/s10755-022-09627-4

Tatum, B. D. (1999). *Why are all the Black kids sitting together in the cafeteria? And other conversations about race.* Basic Books.

Teranishi, R., Suarez-Orozco, C., & Suarez-Orozco, M. (2015). *In the shadows of the ivory tower: Undocumented undergraduates and the liminal state of immigration reform.* The UndocuScholars Project, The Institute for Immigration, Globalization, & Education, University of California, Los Angeles. Retrieved from https://escholarship.org/uc/item/2hq679z4

Tinto, V. (1993). *Leaving college: Rethinking the causes and cures of student attrition* (2nd ed.). University of Chicago Press.

Torres-Olave, B., Torrez, M., Ferguson, K., Bedford, A., Castillo-Lavergne, C., Robles, K., & Chang, A. (2021). Fuera de lugar: Undocumented students, dislocation, and the search for belonging. *Journal of Diversity in Higher Education, 14*(3), 418–428.

Tovar, E. S., & Lee, H. B. (2009). Development and validation of the college mattering inventory with diverse urban college students. *Measurement & Evaluation in Counseling & Development, 42,* 154–178. https://doi.org/10.1177/0748175609344091.

Valdez, Z., & Golash-Boza, T. (2020). Master status or intersectional identity? Undocumented students' sense of belonging on a college campus. *Identities, 27*(4), 481–499. https://doi.org/10.1080/1070289X.2018.1534452

Valenzuela, J. I., Perez, W., Perez, I., Montiel, G. I., & Chaparro, G. (2015). Undocumented students at the community college: Creating institutional capacity. *New Directions for Community Colleges, 172,* 87–96. https://doi.org/10.1002/cc.20166

Yuval-Davis, N. (2011). Belonging and the politics of belonging. In J. McLaughlin, P. Phillimore, & D. Richardson (Eds.), *Contesting recognition: Identity studies in the social sciences.* Palgrave Macmillan. https://doi.org/10.1057/9780230348905_2

7

INVISIBLE EXPERIENCES OF UNDOCUBLACK STUDENTS WITHIN HIGHER EDUCATION

As a young Black undocumented person, I never saw anyone who looked like me in student organizations in high school, undergraduate, or at the graduate level. Even today, I rarely see undocuBlack faces in the national immigrant justice spaces. However, as I began to write this chapter, I thought about the powerful Ted Talk from Chimamanda Ngozi Adichie, in which she details the danger of a single story. In her talk, she notes how every stereotype is rooted in some truth, but the issue with stereotypes is that they tell half-truths. As I explore the undocuBlack experience, I've noticed we have become accustomed to only discussing the Latinx undocumented narrative, which then promotes the idea that the undocumented community is homogeneous. This one-sided narrative unintentionally pushes Black undocumented students back in the shadows. Without a connection to the community, we are rendered invisible. In this chapter, I first position invisibility within the context of undocuBlack immigrants; share the experiences of the participants from the current study; and discuss the implications of invisibility, overcriminalization, and lack of advocacy.

Positioning Invisibility

Sociologists, policymakers, and higher education practitioners have homogenized Blackness in America and have deemed all Black experiences as one, denying the nuances of ethnicity and nationality. Blackness within the United States is influenced by the experiences of those from the diaspora and the baggage that comes from being Black in America. In most Caribbean or African countries, people do not classify themselves by race but by class and culture (Rahier & Hintze, 2014; Charles, 2014). Therefore, when

DOI: 10.4324/9781003442998-9

Black immigrants migrate to the United States, they sometimes struggle to belong within the binaries of Blackness, which is often categorized by racial stratification in America. This positioning affects undocuBlack immigrants because they are first seen as Black, having to fit into Black American culture, while their language and culture might be different.

Black immigrants are also erased from the discussion around unlawful immigration and border security and are subject to racially motivated laws aimed at ceasing the Black population within America, which also result in invisibility (McKanders, 2021). As a result of racial discrimination in America, Black immigrants are overcriminalized through immigration laws and the criminal justice system, which enforce disproportionate deportation of Black immigrants (McKanders, 2021). Because undocuBlack immigrants are omitted or not considered within the policies that affect them, they become invisible, which has consequences such as overcriminalization and lack of advocacy.

At the collegiate level, undocuBlack students have unique challenges to higher education; not only do they face the institutional, structural, and legal barriers that all undocumented students experience, they also face challenges related to invisibility. The undocuBlack participants in the current study experience invisibility within undocumented and Black student spaces on college campuses as the programming, policies, scholarships, and opportunities were not catered to their intersecting identities.

Invisibility Within Undocumented Student Spaces

As previously mentioned, of the 15 participants within the study, only 4 had direct access to a DREAM Center,[1] while 9 had access to undocumented student organizations. The four students who did have access to a DREAM Center reported that they felt invisible within those spaces, noting that the programming and resources were not relevant to them, as they were designed for undocuLatinx students. Greg noted about his experience in his DREAM Center, 'Sometimes people would be surprised because everybody in those clubs are usually Latino and you know, I was like one of the only like Black people in the club or whatever'. According to Taryn, 'the only race[2] that we always saw in TheDream.US space were Hispanics'. Fatima notes, 'I am one of the few Black people in TheDream.US program. . . . You just don't see a Black person and think they are undocumented'. As they were each the only Black student in undocumented spaces, they felt invisible because they did not see themselves represented. However, as is evident, these spaces are important for undocumented students because they serve as important identity-based spaces. Scholars such as Canedo Sanchez and So (2015) have asserted that when undocumented students have access to supportive environments, they have better well-being, and it influences their engagement on campus.

Another finding in the current study as it relates to invisibility in undocumented spaces was that the undocuBlack students who had access to DREAM Centers felt there was a lack of staff representation in those spaces, which also contributed to them feeling invisible. They described feeling invisible as they interacted with faculty, staff, and students. As noted by Rosemary,

> I talked to more people and it seemed like every time I talked to them, they would send me in the same circle of people who would never be able to help me. I just feel like people in general aren't equipped to provide me with the help that I need.

She never felt the staff was knowledgeable enough to help her navigate her precarious situation. Similarly, Taryn accounts her experience with staff being exclusionary in a space for undocumented student: 'Being in the club was very difficult and uncomfortable, and I can see why it made other undocuBlack students feel uncomfortable because you already feel excluded, you already feel scared and now the staff is only speaking Spanish'. Sasha notes, 'I ask staff one question and that person will point me to one direction and another to another direction'. According to Abraham, 'They were not helpful. For instance, I went into the F1-J1 "International Student" office but they did not understand my immigration status. I tried getting an internship and they did not know how to help me' Because staff was not equipped to support them, the undocuBlack participants within the study felt further invisibilized.

This finding is aligned with the research of other scholars such as Freeman et al. (2021), who note that when undocumented students have access to staff and faculty who serve as support for them, it diminishes a sense of marginalization. Additionally, Harris and Patton (2017) and Patton (2005) note that it is important for Black students to have access to faculty and staff who look like them and share similar experiences in order to mitigate feelings of invisibility. Furthermore, in Hall's 2022 study, she noted that undocuBlack students experience an erasure from staff and faculty on college campuses.

Of the nine who joined the undocumented student space[3] that they had access to, they also reported feeling invisible, as they were constantly the only Black person present in those spaces. According to Shannon, 'I participated in [undocumented student club]. I was the only Black student in that club'. Similarly, Arion notes, 'I joined a club for DREAMers, I am the only Black person and I always felt everyone was staring at me'. Participants constantly dealt with not only being the only Black student in those spaces but also being forgotten and unseen because they did not fit the script of an undocumented person. According to Reyna Rivarola and López (2021), the national view or discussion around immigration continues to only advance one image of undocumented students, rendering other groups who 'do not look' undocumented as invisible. Therefore, because the undocuBlack students did not fit the description of an 'undocumented' person, they struggled to feel visible.

Feelings of invisibility within DREAM Centers and undocumented student organizations are discussed in the literature. Salinas Velasco et al. (2015) noted that students who do not identify as Latinx reported feeling that there was a disparity in resources, which contributed to feelings of invisibility within undocumented spaces. Chan (2010) reported that non-Latinx students experience invisibility in undocumented spaces and struggle with having an experience they label as a 'double-edged sword'. Additionally, in Meitzenheimer's 2020 study, the participants divulged that they experience invisibility within undocumented spaces as a result of being Black and undocumented. Meitzenheimer's study is aligned with Huber and Malagon (2007), who also explain that undocumented students with intersecting identities have additional barriers within higher education. This means that undocuBlack students struggle to balance their intersecting identities within undocumented spaces, deeming their existence invisible. However, not only did the undocuBlack participants feel invisible in undocumented spaces, they also felt invisible in Black student spaces because those spaces only catered to the African American experience.

Invisibility Within Black Collegiate Spaces

Because there is a lack of attention to undocuBlack collegiate experiences and Black immigrant higher education experiences, most of the literature that is available centers the Black American experience[4] and ignores undocuBlack students. This erasure is most likely a result of the lack of data about undocuBlack people, which contributes to the invisibility of undocuBlack students. It is important to note that while the scholarship around undocuBlack students is sparse, the literature around the Black immigrant collegiate experiences has increased within the last decade as scholars have paid a close attention to access and belonging for Black immigrant students (see Fries-Britt &Turner, 2001; Griffin & McIntosh, 2015; Hall, 2022; Kent, 2007). For example, Griffin and McIntosh (2015) explored racial and ethnic identity of Black immigrants and their experiences on college campuses; they found that students with intersecting identities influence the way students engage on campus. This finding is evident in other studies as well (Harper & Quaye, 2007; Museus, 2008). Even so, the majority of literature focuses on Black American student experiences rather than undocuBlack student experiences.

Black immigrant students are often categorized as Black Americans, which contributes to further invisibility within Black American student spaces (Carbado et al., 2013). According to Kent (2007), there are fundamental cultural differences between Black international students and Black Americans, yet they are viewed as one in the same for research. While Black immigrants and African American students might share the same racial identity, they do not share the same ethnic sameness (Mwangi & English, 2017).

Additionally, Kim and Lee's (2014) study found that Black immigrant students expressed difficulty connecting with Black American students, which was also notable in the current study. Kent's study asserts that Black immigrant students are in a precarious place: they not only want to connect with Black immigrant students but also find it necessary to connect with Black American students, which creates challenges for them.

As is evident from the aforementioned studies, it was not surprising that undocuBlack participants felt invisible within Black student spaces on college campuses. As mentioned by multiple participants within the current study, the Black experience is not the African American experience alone. Raven stated, 'I find it difficult to connect with African American or African students, because I'm Caribbean and Black'. Additionally, Arion noted, 'I am in the Black Student Union but never go to any of their meetings. I just feel like I am not African American, so I felt distant between Black Americans'. Arion never felt connected to the African American experience even though he lived in America since he was nine years old and considered himself Black. Sasha had similar sentiments:

> I have a difficult time being in those spaces because I don't consider myself African American. I consider myself Black. I think that a lot of people miss that, so I just have a really difficult time navigating a lot of those spaces.

Sasha found Black student spaces difficult to navigate because her Blackness was invisibilized because she was not African American. Furthermore, Rosemary noted, 'With BSU, I felt like it was mostly African Americans, and I feel like I could never relate to African Americans completely either'.

Within Black collegiate spaces, the participants noted that they had to adapt to the African American experience, as the programming, the events, and the gatherings were all centered around the African American experience; there was no account for Black people from the diaspora. This feeling of conformity and the unintentional push to ignore their immigration status contributed to them feeling invisible. The undocuBlack participants within the current study felt uncomfortable disclosing their status to other Black students, so there were no discussions about immigrant identity. As noted by Taryn who was involved in an African student club and a Caribbean student organization, 'Immigration was not brought up; it was laughed about'. The invisible experiences that the participants noted are corroborated by scholars (see Benjamin, 2018; Bryce-Laporte, 1972) who contend that undocuBlack people are invisible. Furthermore, others have shed light on this invisibility within higher education (see Chan, 2010; Hall, 2022; Palmer, 2017; Meitzenheimer, 2020; Russell, 2022; Russell & Cisneros, 2023; Russell & Rivarola, 2023).

Contextualizing Being UndocuBlack Beyond Higher Education

While the undocuBlack participants in the study described their experiences of invisibility within student groups, organizations, and student spaces on college campuses, they also reported that they experienced invisibility by way of the media, the undocumented community as a whole, and the larger Black community as well. That invisibility was further pronounced for undocuBlack students without DACA status as they were often ignored by policies and opportunities. Additionally, all participants noted that they did not see themselves represented within the wider discourse around immigration. One question that provided insight into those two experiences was, '*What does it mean to be undocuBlack?*' While the responses varied for each participant, in some way or another, they all alluded to invisibility.

Invisibility by Way of Underrepresentation of UndocuBlack Stories

Category 1: What does it mean to be undocuBlack?
Category 2: Can you detail the invisibility experience within the community and in college?

Arion said,

> To be undocuBlack to me means being invisible in a world that only recognizes Hispanics as immigrants. And being Black does not help because I constantly get categorized as African American so when it's time to apply for scholarships, I don't fit any of the requirements. It's difficult to fully assimilate to African American culture because I have a culture of my own. Lastly, I always remember that I have to stay grounded because on the exterior I am Black, but internally I know that I am a DACA recipient.
>
> No one expects a Black person to be undocumented. For instance, in the DREAMers club, no one looks like me and when you show up, they don't even know what to do. There's nothing here for me. Not even scholarships because they are mostly for Hispanics.

Arion describes his undocuBlack experience through the lens of his access to resources and the lack of visibility of other undocuBlack people. As a result of his intersecting identities, he was in precarious positions. He recounts that scholarships were never for him. Furthermore, he found it difficult to fully exist within African American culture. So, within the undocumented and Black communities as a whole, he felt invisible. To be undocuBlack meant he was invisible because no one expected an undocumented person to be Black, there were no resources for him, and there were no stories of undocuBlack people.

Shannon said,

> *To be undocuBlack for me means a hyper vigilance through policing myself to avoid police encounters due to double criminalization of both my Blackness and undocumented status. On a more positive note, I believe being undocuBlack allows me to live the Black American experience with an invisible immigrant identity. As a result, I feel like I have a responsibility to bridge the gap between people in the diaspora and on the continent back home since I've experienced living in both settings.*
>
> *Because we are invisible, when I found out that we're five times more likely to be deported, I was like how does that make sense if I'm not being looked at as undocumented? . . . When I was in undocumented spaces, I think some people would not even assume I was undocumented because I remember when I was talking to the coordinator, but she told me like she didn't assume I was undocumented when I walked into the space. I'm the only Black one who sticks out.*

Shannon first details her experience as an undocuBlack person through the lens of criminalization. She felt invisible because she could hide her immigrant identity in plain sight, but she knew that the consequences for her were greater than for her peers. To be undocuBlack meant she was not only invisible but hypervigilant as well.

Taryn said,

> *We are invisible within society's eyes. We can easily assimilate and can be roped into simply being 'Black' – and by that I mean Black American. I think this stems from the fact that many people do not understand that Black is not always equal to Black American. When an undocuBlack person tells a [documented[5]] person about their status, there is much more confusion versus if it was another race. Many people believe that Black only means Black American; however the diaspora is large and touches all corners of the world.*
>
> *I feel very much invisible and sometimes I feel as though my struggles are not heard enough. I often feel torn and in a sense feel like I am living a*

double life. On the outside, people will see me and will not think I am un-documented. When I speak to friends and we discuss international trips, I am ashamed to explain my status because I understand that it will be hard for them to acknowledge and process this situation. In all honesty, I feel as though I will never be able to truly fit in society. I will have to keep scurrying away from the truth like the rats in the NYC subway stations. Scared. Very timid and shy because I felt abnormal. Like, if I miss the tax deadline, I will cry. Everything just feels heightened.

Taryn recounts her undocuBlack experience through her struggles which, as she noted, were because she was invisible. As a result of her invisibility, she felt alone; she was isolated from her friends because she could not share in their experiences. She also notes that the invisibility that she experiences stems from the lack of knowledge that others hold about the undocumented community. For Taryn, to be undocuBlack meant being invisible through-out society, not just within the walls of college campuses or student spaces.

Lucy said,

Almost like you're drowning and a life boat comes and it says citizens only. And then you learn (speaking Haitian Creole) you have to swim to get out, so that's what you learn, like you are the only one that's going to help you like, there is no help. And that's how it felt, and it was very lonely and everybody has advice, but they don't understand. That's the way I can describe it.

We are invisible. When I see stories about undocumented people and the undocumented plight, I don't see Black stories. . . . I also see like a lot of the stories that I see was a lot of undocumented people who were not Black and were also living in like deep blue states right, California and New York and it's like nobody says what it's like to be an undocumented Black person in a red state where there's not going to be a California Dream Act.

Lucy described her undocuBlack experience through imagery. For her, be-ing undocuBlack meant being alone without resources or support. Addi-tionally, because being undocuBlack is so unique, those who attempt to help don't understand how to do so. Furthermore, Lucy's experience with invisibility is pronounced because of the lack of stories she saw in the media. For Lucy, to be undocuBlack meant not only being invisible through media but also being left out for support.

Mitch said,

I mostly see Latinx. They don't see us as undocumented. They think we are refugees. They only think of Latino people. I feel like they exclude us, but I try to stay positive.

Yes, we are invisible. The way people treat Black immigrants or the things they say around us. They just think Latinos are the only ones who could be undocumented; at least, that is how it feels.

Mitch also described his experience in the form of not seeing Black undocumented stories. For him, to be undocuBlack meant not seeing undocuBlack stories. Furthermore, there is a lack of sensitivity around who can be undocumented. To be undocuBlack for Mitch is to be invisible as a result of lack of knowledge from others and the exclusion of undocuBlack immigrant stories.

Teresa said,

Actually I have an example of this, so during the Black Lives Matter movement, it felt like I had to put down my immigration status and just be Black. I remember going to the protests, feeling a bit antsy because I'm like, what if I get arrested at this? It's a different story, for me, not just being Black but also being undocumented or having DACA. This is serious if I'm going. It's like I'm putting my life on the line here in a different way than I think others who were beside me were. So that, during that time it's like I almost just didn't even really think about DACA, and it's interesting that I also felt like it wasn't brought up either. As much as when we're talking about Black lives matter and people were emphasizing different types of Black lives, I didn't necessarily hear Black immigrants being pulled up into the conversation.

I think we are invisible because it took me so long to even find a Black undocumented website and I did, I found an Instagram page for undocu Black Network, maybe like two three years ago. But, especially in the Midwest, barely anything.

Teresa described her undocuBlack experience through an example. For her, being undocuBlack means having to decide which identity is more important in any given moment. During the interview, she recounted her experience navigating the Black Lives Matter protest movement during 2020 and the dilemma she faced with participating. She knew that while the protests were for Black lives, she did not truly feel as Black immigrant lives were represented in that fight. Additionally, she details her invisible experience based on her own lack of access to people and resources. For Teresa, to be undocuBlack is to be invisible even within the Black community as a whole.

Gabby said,

We were like twice rejected because of my skin color first of all, and everything going on in America like all the police brutality things that have been going on. And then being undocumented all the things that are going on against immigrants, people don't want us here because we are Black and because we're undocumented.

For instance, United We Dream[6] have been protesting a lot in DC, but if you look at people protesting, it's Hispanic people, I don't know if I've seen a Black person protesting. Also, when you hear stories about people being undocumented, it's always Hispanic people. People from Latin America.

Gabby recounted her experience about being undocuBlack from a unique perspective. She noted that she felt twice rejected, first because she is Black, then, second, because she is an immigrant. She describes seeing images of immigrants protesting and not seeing a Black person. Additionally, she discusses her invisibility as an ongoing experience that is perpetuated by those leading the fight for immigrant justice. For Gabby, being undocuBlack is to be rejected by those fighting for the marginalized and by the society as a whole.

Rosemary said,

To me, being undocuBlack means having a hidden identity. It means less visibility, sparse resources, and also a lack of community. In higher education especially, it feels as If I am a unicorn and that I am navigating these processes on my own and as the first of my kind. It can feel very lonely.

I don't think we are frequently a part of the conversation, you know. Like we just explored, the needs are a bit different but they're mostly tailored to one demographic and visually not as visible.

Rosemary contends that undocuBlack people are not represented in various spaces. She describes her undocuBlack experience as being hidden, which leads to a lack of resources and community. For her, to be undocuBlack means to be invisible and to be omitted not only from conversations but also from physical spaces designated from undocumented people.

Anthony said,

It is secluded. A lot of work to stay afloat financially. You feel like an outsider. Full of fear, just full of anger, sometimes full of depression. And it's like I just don't know who to talk to about it. . . . It does feel lonely.

The only thing that you know bothers me is that when people talk about undocumented immigrants, it's mostly focused on Hispanics. No one thinks about 'oh there are White people who are also undocumented, Black people who are also undocumented', so you can pretty much be under the bus, most of the time.

Anthony sees his undocuBlack experience as lonely. He never had others to talk to about his status. Furthermore, his invisibility was pronounced because he never saw Black people in the undocumented category. For Anthony, to be undocuBlack meant being invisible and alone.

Raven said,

> *Just a minority, especially living in the United States, everything seems to be against me. I'm one of those people – one of those who fall into so many of those marginalized groups; it's not only that I'm Black, but I am undocumented, you know, a woman, so there's like so many different obstacles.*
>
> *You know if I go to apply for anything and if they're open to undocumented students, it is going to be Latinx students or DACA students and the narrative is always Latinx undocumented people. They don't talk about Black people, so I think that's like if people were to find out right now about my specific status, I think they would all be surprised because I'm Black and because I'm doing so well in school. There is a large majority of undocumented Black people out there, but it's harder to share our stories, because no one talks about it. Even worse – no one asks.*

Raven described her undocuBlack experience with competing intersecting identities, as they place her in delicate positions. Furthermore, her undocuBlack status is invisible because resources are not created for her because she does not have DACA and because she is Black. For Raven, to be undocuBlack means to be without resources and to be invisible.

Abraham said,

> *It means to deal with different identities. One is visible while the other is not – until you deal with the systems of education, banking, housing, healthcare. It is a real impact, and you carry a lot of burden that can have a toll on your mental and physical health. It means advocating for yourself when you may not be visible to different institutions in the U.S. It was emotional and draining.*
>
> *Black undocumented people are not portrayed in the media. It took horrific experiences of the Haitian migrants at the Southern border for others to realize that immigration is a racialized issue. Even within the African immigrant community with legal status, they look down on other immigrants who are undocumented/without legal status.*

Abraham did not see stories of undocuBlack people; his own story was not reflected in the media, the Black community or the undocumented community. For Abraham, to be undocuBlack meant to balance his intersecting identities while also being invisible through the eyes of society.

Sasha said,

> *First, I feel like anytime I've spoken with people, they don't know that Black people can be immigrants and I'm like y'all know Black people exist outside of America right? It's interesting that people don't think about it, but when you think about how the media portrays immigration, it makes sense as to why the thought wouldn't even occur to them. . . . It's a difficult space to navigate. 2020 being one of the hardest years for me ever. And it was like I'm always going to be undocumented and I'm always going to be reminded because whether it's an election year, or whatever is going on, like the Supreme Court is going to rule on DACA.*
>
> *We are invisible. I work with a national org. I'm not sure if you're familiar with BAJI.[7] So I work with them, so I'm in spaces where it's okay we're here, we're alive, but then I go to a conference and we [undocuBlack people] are little specks of pepper. We're definitely ignored. I am usually one of five Black people in the room and sometimes the others are workers. We are also underrepresented for sure.*

From Sasha's perspective, she experienced invisibility even when she was in spaces for undocumented people. For her, being undocuBlack meant being invisible in spaces for undocumented people and constantly balancing the roller coaster of emotions that comes with DACA's legal battles.

Greg said,

> *I feel the best way of saying it is like you don't have a home. You don't belong anywhere right, because it's like you know as much as I hate to say it out loud, I really don't know what Togo is like, I can't visit there. But at the same time I'm from there. I think that's like the biggest intersection because it's like being Black, like even the Black Americans here are excluded from the community, they kind of are outside of it. So that makes it triplely so because I'm not even from the U.S. I'm not even from Africa, like I don't belong anywhere in the world. I'm a vagabond.*
>
> *We are invisible. Like I said, a lot of the events in [club][8] became very themed towards like Latinx culture and heritage. I would say being Black and undocumented is 100% invisible inside the undocumented community, like 100%. It feels lonely.*

For Greg, he saw his undocuBlack experience through yearning to belong. He did not feel like he belonged anywhere. Furthermore, in undocumented student spaces, the events were centered around the Latinx experience. For Greg, to be undocuBlack meant being a vagabond and being invisible in undocumented spaces.

Fatima said,

> I am Black at a HBCU so I fit into the narrative, so my status is not pronounced on campus. In TheDream.US group, it is clear that my status is pronounced because I am one of the only Black people in that group.
>
> We are invisible because I don't hear about Black undocumented people too much.

Fatima's response to being undocuBlack was rooted in her experience attending an HBCU. Because she was at an HBCU, she was constantly surrounded by Black students, so she did not have to regularly think of her race. However, as she notes, in undocumented spaces, she felt her identity as an immigrant was on display. For Fatima, being undocuBlack meant invisibility because of the lack of Black immigrant stories.

Darius said,

> I feel like I am able to blend in with Black people and not be recognized as undocumented. But, I know immigration is only a Black issue if we make it a Black issue so I started announcing in spaces that I'm undocumented. If I didn't do that, like everyone would just see me as a Black American. . . . In those spaces where I announce it, people still don't understand it, and I have to continuously explain it. For instance, I have a boss who always says, 'we are going to get your papers fixed'. He just does not understand it. With Black people, they don't understand it either.
>
> We are invisible because there is a white supremacy view of immigration that trickles into a lot of organizations. It starts with the media and the images they portray. They even dehumanize Haitian immigrants more.

Darius details his undocuBlack experience as being invisible. In Black spaces, they don't understand how he could possibly be undocumented, and in undocumented spaces, they don't understand how he could be Black. For Darius, being undocuBlack means being invisible because people are unaware of the immigrant landscape.

Summary

The quotes noted earlier represent the sentiments from participants who emphasized that one of the main reasons they feel invisible is because undocuBlack stories are unknown. They constantly felt that they did not belong to anywhere, which contributed to feelings of invisibility. The invisibility finding within the undocumented community is corroborated throughout the literature (see Anderson, 2015; Benjamin, 2018; Bryce-Laporte, 1972; Hall, 2022; Russell, 2022) and within higher education (see Chan, 2010; Palmer, 2017; Meitzenheimer, 2020). Essentially, to be undocuBlack is to be invisible and to see a lack of representation of their stories.

Invisibility by Way of Access to Resources and Alienation of the UnDACAmented

Another finding that pointed to the participants feeling invisible was their experiences with lack of access to resources or their own alienation because they did not have DACA status. Of the 15 participants, 7 did not have DACA and 1 was a TPS holder. Those without DACA felt even more invisible because they could not access the resources or communities that those with DACA status had. This type of invisibility compounded with being Black produced further isolation for the unDACAmented[9] students. This theme was realized through questions such as: '*What challenges or obstacles did you face as an undocuBlack college student?*' and '*What did it mean to use or not use support services for undocumented students?*' The undocuBlack participants within the current study noticed how forgotten they were by administrators, students, staff, and faculty on their campuses.

What Challenges or Obstacles Did You Face as an UndocuBlack College Student?

Category 1: UndocuBlack Students Without DACA Status

Raven said,

> *A lot of these challenges, I would not be facing if I was not undocumented and Black. . . . Not being able to have a job. Not being able to do summer programs, because you need to at least have DACA to do a summer program. All of the resources were mostly for DACA students, so I don't personally feel comfortable joining programs.[10] But, I have talked to people from those programs, but they are not helpful to me. They help students with DACA, but they can't help undocumented students. There's just a big divide between DACA and completely undocumented students.*

The obstacles and challenges that Raven faced were not only due to her being Black and undocumented, but not having DACA status also added compounded struggles for her. Without DACA status, there were no specialized resources or support for her on her campus. Not only did she feel uncomfortable interacting with those who were undocumented, but she never felt supported by faculty or staff as well. Therefore, as a result of not having DACA, her salient identities made her even more invisible.

Anthony said,

> I just don't know the resources that I need, apart from the Dream Center. I don't think there's like any other resources out there and then the information about what is going on federal wise about immigration, and then also mental health support and all that. Like, having to take six months off from school to make some money. Or when I hear friends talk about applying for financial aid. I just do one day at a time.

The challenges and obstacles that Anthony faced were due to not having additional resources on his campus other than the DREAM Center. He noted that he did not know where to go for support or how to access certain services that he thought were necessary for his persistence. Without the support, he had to take months off school to afford his education, which affects the way he navigates his college journey. Therefore, as a result of being undocuBlack and without DACA status, he faced additional barriers to resources, a theme that was common among those without DACA status.

Rosemary said,

> Looking for resources and then they're all for Latinx people. Also, not having a network of support. I don't think I got past them per se, I just kind of accepted that that was going to be my situation, something that I was just going to deal with. The thing is like DACA vs undocumented – that's what I run into a lot, and it discourages me. I think I've seen different people that I would have wanted to reach out to, but then I realized that they do have DACA, and then I realized that our paths have been different.

The barriers and challenges that Rosemary experienced were also specific to her not having DACA status. Again, Rosemary recounts her tiresome journey having to navigate being undocuBlack and without DACA, which made her collegiate experience burdensome and lonely. Additionally, she saw those with DACA status as having an easier path to success. Being un-DACAmented contributed to Rosemary feeling invisible.

Abraham said,

> I am not sure, because for me like when you see me, you know I am Black, you don't know if I am undocumented. No access to healthcare or not being able

to get certain services. And so, for me, my being Black is like the forefront of all these identities. And yeah like be undocumented has really concrete effects, but also being Black like I mentioned, you can see the way people speak to you. May have these microaggressions. You will get underestimated so like those are more intangible things right. But, when it comes to the undocumented, it is tangible – like it's real life, you cannot drive, you cannot go to a certain event because you don't have an ID, or get a job because of no social security number. When it comes to being Black, it is more intense for men. There are also mental effects, like a psychological effect on you.

For Abraham, he saw his salient identities impact his day-to-day life. His undocumented status limited his access to healthcare, a driver's license, and access to aid. Being Black impacted the way others treated him, the way they spoke to him, or regarded him in conversations. He also notes that his gender adds a layer of difficulty to being undocuBlack. Abraham's invisibility was a double-edge sword because one status others could see and the others, they could not. However, both identities contributed to the lack of access he had to resources, which was due, in part, to his invisibility.

Gabby said,

I would say, my main challenges were my mental health. And then I would want to go to counseling but not many people understand what I go through. I am still struggling through them every single day, but sleep helps. . . . Scholarships that I came across were specifically for Hispanic undocumented people or people with DACA; I don't think I saw one that was for Black undocumented people.

According to Gabby, the obstacles that she encountered were related to her mental health[11] and non-DACA status. As a result of her undocumented status, she wanted to access mental health services but could not find them. This was partly because she was isolated from the undocumented community because she did not have DACA. As Gabby noted, she did not notice scholarships for Black undocumented students and only for her Latinx peers. Again, her invisibility contributed to her lack of access to resources.

Shannon said,

I started doing advocacy around creating fellowships for undocumented students, specifically those who don't have DACA because programming at the Dream Center or other undocumented spaces are geared towards DACA folks. I started to feel awkward because everybody else had DACA, so it made me feel somewhat isolated. . . . I could barely focus on graduating. Not having DACA. Housing. Money.

Shannon felt isolated because she did not have DACA. Therefore, she had to find ways to advocate for students without DACA so that they could have access to resources. Shannon struggled because she did not have DACA. Her invisibility as an undocuBlack person limited her access to resources, such as scholarships, and her non-DACA status led to further isolation from those resources.

Category 2: UndocuBlack Students With DACA Status

While most of the participants without DACA status expressed their struggles and obstacles from the perspective of being without DACA, those with DACA status also struggled to access resources and support. From their responses, it is clear that they faced additional barriers to successfully persisting within higher education because of their undocuBlack identities. One of the consequences of this invisibility is that undocuBlack students not only are further isolated from the community but also have even more limitations to access resources.

What Challenges or Obstacles Did You Face as an UndocuBlack College Student?

One of the major themes noted in obstacles and barriers that participants faced was their access to scholarships. According to Teresa,

> *The lack of representation I feel like when you look at the people when it's time to talk about being undocumented, the people represented usually aren't Black. When I was handed the scholarship list there were a lot of the scholarships that said, for Latino students, so that is discouraging, so the representation it's very lacking. I'm the only Black DACA student that I know on this campus. To get past the obstacles I would say just remaining positive, I'm really big in my faith.*

For Teresa, the scholarships for undocumented students were only for Latinx students. Even though she had the DACA status, she still did not have access to scholarships for undocumented students because the criteria were explicit in who could apply. She also notes that there was a lack of representation within the undocumented community and she rarely saw Black undocumented people.

Similar to Teresa, Arion noted that he struggled to find scholarships for undocuBlack students. Arion said,

> *I would say, trying to find scholarships that's been one of the hardest things. Like when I'm from Jamaica looking up scholarships, they'll have it for Hispanics and I'm just like, but Hispanics aren't the only one that's undocumented. They forget about us.*

Arion's lack of access to resources was due to being Black and undocumented.

Another major barrier was the stress related to DACA status and the legal battles it faced in court. According to Darius when asked, *'what challenges or obstacles did you face as an undocuBlack college student?'*,

> *Feeling isolated and not having access to financial aid. It was stressful every semester knowing I had to fork out money to pay for school. I also would get into those funks. It was easier to navigate the isolation part because I always knew I was undocumented, so I just knew there were certain things I could not do. The financial aid and funk was harder to overcome because I just had to be okay with my mother paying and I had to be fine with doing the research to fill out DACA.*

For Darius, he struggled with isolation, lack of access to financial aid, the stress of filling out his DACA application, and the 'funk' he would get into each semester.

Similarly, Taryn noted,

> *When Trump came into the presidency, it was hard. DACA was rescinded, and I did not have money to renew mine. Also, I had an eviction notice, so it was hard to focus on school.*

Taryn had to deal with the constant legal battles of DACA and the uncertainty that contributed to her being successful in college.

Similarly, Greg struggled with DACA being contested in the courts. He said,

> *So the challenges and obstacles that I faced as an undocuBlack student in college is that I had this internal pressure of hey if I mess up, that's it for me. Also, there was a lot of uncertainty with DACA. I got past it because of the love and support from my family and friends.*

Others like Sasha and Lucy noted they felt alone and lacked access to community. According to Sasha,

> *Funding would be the first one. I think the second one would just be trying to find a space, like I think about all the people who come into college right out of high school and I'm doing it at a time where it's like I know myself, I've advocated for myself, life is very different for me. So, for me it's difficult because I've been at [university][12] for a year, and I haven't met anyone who's openly undocumented or DACAmented. I think my third biggest thing is that I think that it should be on the college to have that resource*

of communities for students so they can find their own communities. Work in a way to have that community there and then you find your community within that community. I get past these obstacles because of my mentor.

And Lucy said,

Mostly, like I mentioned, I feel alone, you know people automatically when they see you they don't automatically think you don't have papers, so you have to answer a lot of questions of why.

Summary

Ultimately, as a result of being undocuBlack, the participants felt invisible because they could not access resources such as scholarships, fellowships, and additional funding opportunities that Latinx undocumented students had access to. For participants without DACA, they experienced further isolation from the community and an even harder time accessing scholarships that were available to students with DACA.

Conclusions and Implications of Invisibility

Overall, the undocuBlack participants in the current study felt invisible by way of the undocumented spaces they attempted to occupy, the tone-deaf interactions they had with faculty and staff, the lack of narrative representation within the media, and the ostracization they dealt within Black native spaces on campuses.

While it is important to acknowledge the invisibility that the undocuBlack students in this study experienced, it is also essential to comprehend the implications of invisibility. I assert that the implications of invisibility are larger than the lack of access to resources; invisibility also leads to overcriminalization and lack of advocacy for undocuBlack immigrants, which is detrimental to undocuBlack students' successful persistence within higher education. Overcriminalization and lack of advocacy have a direct impact on Black immigrants and their livelihood and belonging in America. Without addressing these implications, Black immigrants will continue to suffer at the hands of immigration policies more than any other immigrant community.

Invisibility and Criminalization

Tanya Golash-Boza (2017) is a notable scholar who has pointed out how the invisibility of Black immigrants leads to criminalization; she argues that

Black immigrants are erased from the discussion of mass incarceration, but they bear the consequences of the system. In her 2017 study, she interviewed 24 Black immigrants, specifically Jamaicans and Dominicans, with a goal of understanding how mass incarceration affects Black male immigrants. Her article asserts that immigration enforcement on Black immigrants is at the intersection of anti-Black racism and notes that the policies disproportionately harm Black immigrants. This study is important to analyze because it points to the consequences that are a result of invisibility among Black immigrants. If policymakers are not aware that undocuBlack immigrants exist, they will continue to be disproportionately affected by immigration policies, which then will affect their trajectories within higher education.

The aforementioned study is not the only scholarly work that has attempted to display the implications of invisibility of undocuBlack immigrants. Benjamin (2018) contended that Blackness has implicit and explicit consequences for Black immigrants. Meitzenheimer (2020) asserted that undocuBlack immigrants are overpoliced because of being Black and immigrants. Furthermore, in Johnson's 2005 article, 'The Case for African American and Latina/o Cooperation in Challenging Racial Profiling in Law Enforcement', he contended that Black immigrants are more likely to be stripped, detained, or unlawfully have their immigration status questioned because of their Blackness. Lipscombe et al. (2016) noted that Black immigrants face criminalization at a higher rate than their Latinx counterparts. Furthermore, Miller (2002) claims that immigration and mass incarceration are connected and produce negative consequences for Black immigrants.

The implications of invisibility can be analyzed through the policies of various administrations. Under former President Barack Obama, one in three Black immigrants were deported on criminal grounds (Cházaro, 2016). The Trump administration specifically implemented policies that were detrimental to immigrants of color. His administration deported African immigrants at a higher rate than any other immigrant group, where removals jumped by '140% to 1815 people removed in 2017, from 756 in 2016' (The State of the Immigration Courts, n.d.). Trump also instituted a travel ban that targeted African countries and made additional attempts to terminate Temporary Protected Status for immigrants from countries with majority-Black populations, such as Haiti. In fact, as one of the participants who I interviewed stated, 'Haitian immigrants are the cheapest to deport, so they do it to us all the time'.

Even though Black immigrants only make up about 9% of the undocumented population, they represent 20% of immigrants facing deportation due to criminal offenses (Coalition commends congressional leaders for letter to Biden demanding relief for Black immigrants, 2023). This large disparity is a result of Black immigrants experiencing racism and discrimination under administrative policies. Furthermore, Black immigrants are constantly denied the right to asylum (Coalition commends congressional leaders for letter to Biden demanding relief for Black immigrants, 2023).

The scholarship that currently exists corroborates the dangers of invisibility and the impact it has on undocuBlack immigrants, such as overcriminalization. It is necessary for scholars, policymakers, and practitioners to work to dismantle the laws and policies that push Black immigrants to be invisible and vulnerable within the criminal justice and immigration systems. 'Ultimately, undocuBlack people need to be visible within the community and in the narratives being centered because of historical oppression and exclusion that have led to disproportionate deportation rates for Black immigrants' (Russell, 2022, p. 156).

Invisibility and Lack of Advocacy

Not only is the overcriminalization an implication of invisibility but so is the lack of advocacy. Race is tied to exclusion and racial hierarchy within America, which produces a lack of advocacy for Black undocumented people. Without visibility, undocuBlack immigrants will experience a lack of advocacy regarding resources and support services, and institutional, state, and federal policies will exclude them. Without resources, undocuBlack immigrants will not be able to successfully persist within higher education. This lack of advocacy was evident in the current study as the participants noted that the programming and events that the DREAM Centers held were never focused on the undocuBlack narrative; scholarships available for undocumented students were specific to Latinx or DACAmented students; and undocuBlack students did not have strong relationships with faculty, staff, and other students. Due to the invisibility of undocuBlack immigrants, there is a lack of advocacy on all levels: institutional, state, and federal.

The research is clear that once staff, faculty, and others understand the experiences of undocumented students, they can better support and advocate for them (Cervantes et al., 2015; Chen & Rhoads, 2016). Scholars such as Teranishi et al. (2015) have asserted that undocumented students want to have a representation on campus. As noted by Enriquez (2011), undocumented students depend on peers as networks for support. Furthermore, access to peers promotes resources. Scholars have noted that the relationships with faculty and staff are important for undocumented students and lead to advocacy for resources (Suárez-Orozco et al., 2015). Faculty and staff play crucial roles in providing safety and spaces of empowerment for undocumented students (Cisneros et al., 2022). However, the participants in the current study noted that they rarely had access to staff or faculty who knew how to support them with questions regarding their immigration status. People who interact with undocumented students often do not know the needs of the students (Enriquez et al., 2019). I argue that this experience demonstrates how the invisibility of this group further marginalizes them and excludes them from policies at the institutional, state, and federal levels that could benefit them.

Ultimately, this invisibility finding showcases that undocuBlack students within higher education face additional struggles as a result of their salient identities. The undocuBlack participants within the current study demonstrate the difficulties they experienced within undocumented student and Black student spaces on college campuses, whether through their lack of access to scholarships, faculty, staff, or programming geared to their experiences. They also struggled within the larger undocumented and Black communities as a whole because they did not see their stories represented. Representation leads to advocacy for internships, scholarships, programming, opportunities, and many more resources.

Additionally, the media also perpetuates an immigrant narrative that erases undocuBlack people. That erasure or lack of visibility leads to over-criminalization through immigration policies and within the criminal justice system. The invisibility of the undocuBlack community also leads to a lack of advocacy because no one knows or discusses this group. The current study is necessary because it sheds light on these issues and exhibits the need to amplify undocuBlack immigrant voices. The amplification of these voices can lead to access to resources, change in immigration and criminal justice policies, and better institutional policies, increasing undocuBlack immigrants' successful transition and success within higher education.

Consequently, the experiences noted by the participants in the current study point to the need for additional research around undocuBlack students' higher education experiences, which will lead to a greater understanding of undocuBlack experiences within Black native spaces on college campuses. Therefore, now more than ever, it is imperative that undocuBlack immigrant student voices are centered so that policymakers, scholars, practitioners, and faculty understand the nuances of how to support this group – the marginalized within the marginalized. According to Smith (2020), centralizing Black narratives is important because of the continuous divisive portrayal of Black immigrants. After all, Black undocumented college students represent close to 13% of the undocumented students enrolled in higher education (American Immigration Council & PAHEI, 2023). If the experiences of undocuBlack immigrant students are amplified, then teachers, faculty, administrators, scholars, policymakers, and practitioners will be able to create a sense of community for Black immigrants, which will lead to the visibility for undocuBlack students on college campuses across the United States. The current study should provide a meaningful addition to the current literature around the undocuBlack experience on college campuses.

Notes

1. DREAM Centers are considered physical safe spaces on college campuses that exist for members within the undocumented community to exist freely. According to Cisneros and Reyna Rivarola (2020), USRCs are physical spaces that serve as resources for undocumented students on higher education campuses.
2. Hispanic is not a race, but I wanted to keep the participant's exact quote.
3. Not DREAM Centers but an undocumented student organization on their campus.
4. This is not to suggest that there is a plethora of literature about Black American students.
5. The participant used the phrase 'non undocumented'.
6. United We Dream is the largest immigrant youth-led network in the country.
7. Black Alliance for Just Immigration.
8. I omitted the name of the student club that the participant referenced since it is a specific club within that particular state.
9. I am identifying those without DACA status as unDACAmented – a term that has not been widely accepted by scholars, but I will use it interchangeably throughout this chapter.
10. The participant was referring to undocumented support organizations.
11. A lack of access to mental health support was a theme among the undocuBlack participants within the study but not a focal point of this book.
12. The name of the university omitted for privacy purposes.

References

American Immigration Council & PAHEI. (2023, August 8). *Undocumented students in higher education.* Presidents' Alliance on Higher Education and Immigration. Retrieved from www.higheredimmigrationportal.org/research/undocumented-students-in-higher-education-updated-march-2021/.

Anderson, M. (2015, April 9). *A rising share of the U.S. Black population is foreign born.* Pew Research Center. Retrieved from www.pewresearch.org/social-trends/2015/04/09/a-rising-share-of-the-u-s-black-population-is-foreign-born/.

Benjamin, T. (2018). *Black removal and invisibility: At the intersections of race and citizenship in the 21st century* [Doctoral dissertation, University of Maryland]. UMD Theses and Dissertations. Retrieved from https://drum.lib.umd.edu/handle/1903/21260.

Bryce-Laporte, R. (1972). Black immigrants. *Journal of Black Studies, 3*(1), 29–56. https://doi.org/10.1177/002193477200300103

Carbado, D. W., Crenshaw, K. W., Mays, V. M., & Tomlinson, B. (2013). Intersectionality: Mapping the movements of a theory. *Du Bois Review: Social Science Research on Race, 10*(2), 303–312. https://doi.org/10.1017/s1742058x13000349

Cervantes, J., Minero, L., & Brito, E. (2015). Tales of survival 101 for undocumented Latina/o immigrant university students: Commentary and recommendations from qualitative interviews. *Journal of Latina/O Psychology, 3*(4), 224–238. https://doi.org/10.1037/lat0000032

Charles, C. (2014). Being Black twice. In *Problematizing blackness: Self ethnographies by black immigrants to the United States/edited by Percy Claude Hintzen and Jean Muteba Rahier.* essay, Routledge.

Chan, B. (2010). Not just a Latino issue: Undocumented students in higher education. *Journal of College Admission, 206,* 29–31.

Cházaro, A. (2016). Challenging the "Criminal Alien" paradigm. *UCLA Law Review, 63*(594).

Chen, A. C., & Rhoads, R. A. (2016). Undocumented student allies and transformative resistance: An ethnographic case study. *The Review of Higher Education, 39*(4), 515–542. https://doi.org/10.1353/rhe.2016.0033.

Cisneros, J., & Reyna Rivarola, A. R. (2020). Undocumented student resource centers. *Journal of College Student Development, 61*(5), 658–662. https://doi.org/10.1353/csd.2020.0064

Cisneros, J., Valdivia, D., Reyna Rivarola, A. R., & Russell, F. (2022). "I'm here to fight along with you": Undocumented student resource centers creating possibilities. *Journal of Diversity in Higher Education, 15*(5), 607–616. https://doi.org/10.1037/dhe0000355

Coalition commends congressional leaders for letter to Biden demanding relief for Black immigrants. (2023, June 23).

Enriquez, L. E. (2011). "Because we feel the pressure and we also feel the support": Examining the educational success of undocumented immigrant Latina/o students. *Harvard Educational Review, 81,* 476–500. https://doi.org/10.17763/haer.81.3.w7k703q050143762

Enriquez, L., Morales Hernandez, M., Millán, D., & Vazquez Vera, D. (2019). Mediating illegality: Federal, state, and institutional policies in the educational experiences of undocumented college students. *Law & Social Inquiry, 44*(3), 679–703. https://doi.org/10.1017/lsi.2018.16

Freeman, R., Varelas, D. I., & Castillo, D. (2021). Building critical bridges: The role of university presidents in collaborating with undocumented student activists. *Journal of College Access, 6*(2).

Fries-Britt, S. L., & Turner, B. (2001). Facing stereotypes: A case study of Black students on a White campus. *Journal of College Student Development, 42*(5), 420–429.

Golash-Boza, T. (2017). Structural racism, criminalization, and pathways to deportation for Dominican and Jamaican men in the United States. *Social Justice, 44*(2–3 (148)), 137–162. Retrieved from www.jstor.org/stable/26538385.

Griffin, K., & McIntosh, K. (2015). Finding a fit: Understanding Black immigrant students' engagement in campus activities. *Journal of College Student Development, 56*(3), 243–260. https://doi.org/10.1353/csd.2015.0025.

Hall, K. (2022). Undocumented Black students and hermeneutical injustice: Higher education's role in leaving them out of the undocumented conversation. *Journal of First-Generation Student Success, 2*(3), 143–160. https://doi.org/10.1080/26906015.2022.2115327

Harper, S., & Quaye, S. J. (2007). Student organizations as venues for Black identity expression and development among African American male student leaders. *Journal of College Student Development, 48,* 127–144.

Harris, J. C., & Patton, L. D. (2017). The challenges and triumphs in addressing students' intersectional identities for Black culture centers. *Journal of Diversity in Higher Education, 10*(4), 334–349. https://doi.org/10.1037/dhe0000047

Huber, P., & Malagon, C. (2007). Silenced struggles: The experiences of Latina and Latino undocumented college students in California. *The Nevada Journal, 7,* 841–861.

Johnson, K. R. (2005). African American and Latina/o cooperation in challenging racial profiling. *Neither Enemies nor Friends*, 247–263. https://doi.org/10.1057/9781403982636_13

Kent, M. M. (2007). Immigration and America's Black population. *Population Reference Bureau*, 62(4), 3–16.

Kim, Y., & Lee, D. (2014). Internalized model minority myth, Asian values, and help-seeking attitudes among Asian American students. *Cultural Diversity & Ethnic Minority Psychology*, 20, 98–106. https://doi.org/10.1037/a0033351

Lipscombe, C., Trostle, J., & Zheng, K. (2016). *The state of black immigrants part I: A statistical portrait of black immigrants in the United States*. Black Alliance for Just Immigration (BAJI).

McKanders, K. M. (2021). Immigration and racial justice: Enforcing the borders of Blackness. *HeinOnline*.

Meitzenheimer, B. (2020). *"Know that we exist": Storytelling as self-making for undocuBlack students* [Master's thesis, University of California, Los Angeles]. UCLA Electronic Theses and Dissertations. Retrieved from https://escholarship.org/uc/item/7bm6367f.

Miller, T. (2002). The impact of mass incarceration on immigration policy. In M. Mauer & M. Chesney (Eds.), *Invisible punishment: The collateral consequences of mass incarceration*. New Press.

Museus, S. D. (2008). The role of ethnic student organizations in fostering African American and Asian American students' cultural adjustment and membership at predominantly White institutions. *Journal of College Student Development*, 49, 568–586.

Mwangi, C., & English, S. (2017). Being Black (and) immigrant students: When race, ethnicity, and nativity collide. *International Journal of Multicultural Education*, 19(2), 100. https://doi.org/10.18251/ijme.v19i2.1317

Palmer, B. J. (2017). The crossroads: Being black, immigrant, and undocumented in the era of #blacklivesmatter. *Georgetown Journal of Law & Modern Critical Race Perspectives*, 9(1), 99–121.

Patton, L. D. (2005). Power to the people! Black student protest and the emergence of Black culture centers. In F. L. Hord (Ed.), *Black culture centers: Politics of survival and identity* (pp. 151–163). Third World Press.

Rahier, J. M., & Hintzen, P. C. (2014). *Problematizing Blackness: Self ethnographies by black immigrants to the United States/edited by Percy Claude Hintzen and Jean Muteba Rahier*. Routledge.

Reyna Rivarola, A., & López, G. (2021). Moscas, metiches, and methodologies: Exploring power, subjectivity, and voice when researching the undocumented. *International Journal of Qualitative Studies in Education*, 34(8), 733–745. https://doi.org/10.1080/09518398.2021.1930262

Russell, F. (2022). *The invisibility of undocuBlack students within the undocumented community in higher education* [Doctoral dissertation, Temple University]. Theses and Dissertations. https://doi.org/10.34944/dspace/7734

Russell, F., & Cisneros, J. (2023). The (un)embraced: The experiences of Black undocumented students on college campuses. *Journal of Diversity in Higher Education*. Advance online publication. https://doi.org/10.1037/dhe0000523

Russell, F. S., & Rivarola, A. R. R. (2023). What does it mean to be undocuBlack? exploring the double invisibility of black undocumented immigrant students in U.S. colleges and universities. *New Directions for Higher Education*, 1–16. https://doi.org/10.1002/he.20480

Salinas Velasco, C., Mazumder, T., & Enriquez, L. (2015). "It's not just a Latino issue": Policy recommendations to better support a racially diverse population of undocumented students. *Interactions: UCLA Journal of Education and Information Studies, 11*(1), 1–11. https://doi.org/10.5070/D4111024378

Sanchez, R. E., & So, M. L. (2015). UC Berkeley's undocumented student program: Holistic strategies for undocumented student equitable success across Higher Education. *Harvard Educational Review, 85*(3), 464–477. https://doi.org/10.17763/0017-8055.85.3.464

Smith, P. (2020). Silencing invisibility: Toward a framework for black immigrant literacies. *Teachers College Record: The Voice of Scholarship in Education, 122*(13), 1–42. https://doi.org/10.1177/016146812012201301

The state of the immigration courts: Trump leaves Biden 1.3 million case backlog in immigration courts trac immigration report. Perma.cc. (n.d.). Retrieved from https://perma.cc/3MVE-89RU.

Suárez-Orozco, C., Katsiaficas, D., Birchall, O., Alcantar, C. M., Hernandez, E., Garcia, Y., Michikyan, M., Cerda, J., & Teranishi, R. T. (2015). Undocumented undergraduates on college campuses: Understanding their challenges and assets and what it takes to make a undocufriendly campus. *Harvard Educational Review, 85*(3), 427–465. https://doi.org/10.17763/0017-8055.85.3. 427

Teranishi, R., Suárez-Orozco, C., & Suárez-Orozco, M. (2015). *In the shadows of the ivory tower: Undocumented undergraduates and the liminal state of immigration reform.* The Institute for Immigration, Globalization, and Education. Retrieved from www.undocuscholars.org/assets/undocus cholarsreport2016.pdf.

8

AMPLIFY UNDOCUBLACK VOICES

It was difficult to interview people who had stories similar to my own because it meant I was reliving my traumas, and they too had to dig deep to discuss the pain and the rejection they have experienced as undocuBlack people. Simultaneously, it was exciting because I knew it meant that a study centered around the experiences of undocuBlack immigrants could penetrate the literature, the media, the classrooms, the policy centers, and the higher education space. The participants also knew that their stories were important to tell because they had not seen undocuBlack representation within the immigrant discourse. The undocuBlack participants within the current study had not only defied all odds to make it to higher education but they were also persisting or had successfully persisted. Similar to all undocumented students, the undocuBlack participants in this study were resilient, hopeful, brilliant, and tenacious. They were open and brave in sharing their stories with me and you.

In honoring them, this chapter is dedicated to providing actionable steps that we can all take to amplify their voices. Without undocuBlack voices, policymakers and higher education institutions will remain uninformed about the undocumented community. We have a responsibility to create a visibility around the undocuBlack experience. Therefore, if we (policymakers, researchers, scholars, educators, higher education practitioners, and other students) aim to amplify undocuBlack voices, we will achieve:

1) a better understanding of the diversity of the undocumented community,
2) a comprehension of the gaps in the literature, which erase the racialized experiences of undocuBlack immigrants and the ability to address those gaps,

DOI: 10.4324/9781003442998-10

3) an acknowledgment of the connection between the criminal justice system and immigration policies, and
4) better institutional policies that will contribute to the persistence of undocuBlack students within higher education.

In this chapter, I first share responses from participants about what they want practitioners, scholars, educators, and policymakers to know about how race and status affected their college experience. Second, I provide three recommendations on how we amplify undocuBlack voices. Then, I highlight three organizations doing impactful work to support undocuBlack immigrants: Black Alliance for Just Immigration (BAJI), African Communities Together (ACT), and the UndocuBlack Network. Finally, I challenge scholars, policymakers, and higher education practitioners to not only acknowledge undocuBlack immigrants but also amplify their voices in their work.

What Else Do You Want Us to Know?

One final insight that the participants in the study wanted to share was a message to those working toward immigrant justice. One of the last questions I asked all participants was: *Is there anything else you want to share about how race and immigration status affected your college experience?* Two (Sasha and Darius) of the 15 participants noted that they felt they had shared everything already, but 13 of them did share, and next, I share their responses with a summary for each. The undocuBlack participants in this study were not a monolith, and it shows in their responses.

Raven, College Student, 20 Years Old, Undocumented

> *I've always been told not to share my story, but I really do feel it's important for us to share our stories. You're the first Black undocumented person I've ever spoken. . . . I was actually talking to my therapist in our last meeting and she was like you know you should try to find other people that are in the same situation because they can be really good support system, and that's so true but it's like one, I don't know any because no one is sharing their story, you know and like there are also Hispanic undocumented students but they still do not share the same exact experiences as me. I am in a space where I need to have a support system with people that I feel like I can really relate to and being undocumented and Black would be a plus for me because there's so many different layers of being undocumented.*

When I first got to speak to Raven, I was nervous and delighted because she was from Jamaica. As an undocuBlack Jamaican myself, I had never met anyone else who shared an origin country with me and who was also undocumented. Interestingly enough, Raven had also never met another undocumented Jamaican, and she was eager to share her story with me, even though she had been advised not to do so because of the possible consequences. What Raven wanted us to know was that we (policymakers, practitioners, educators, and scholars) should amplify undocuBlack voices. Her story demonstrated durability and resolve to continue to aim for a world in which she exists as freely as her peers. Students like Raven need higher education practitioners who can adequately advise them throughout their collegiate experience.

Abraham, College Graduate, 26 Years Old, Undocumented

> *Black undocumented people are not known. Being Black makes you more vulnerable to police violence. Once you are a victim of police violence, it's even hard for us to rebel or like to file a complaint or go to court, because you are scared they will even deport you. I always have to think, 'what is my life going to be', because, regardless, even if I become legal today, I'm still going to have those obstacles as a Black man. I'll say going back to what I was saying earlier, just being undocumented, you have tangible effects, whereas being Black is a lot of things that are also intangible, like mental health. A lot of things affect our community.*

Abraham had a tremendous story because he navigated through undergraduate and graduate school without DACA and without much support from the undocumented or Black American communities. His strength was obvious in his accomplishments and also was his no-nonsense attitude to keep going even without the resources that he needed. Abraham was adamant that we should uplight undocuBlack stories and demonstrate the discrepancies within the criminal justice and immigration systems. His story, in so many ways, represents the marginalized within the marginalized.

Lucy, College Graduate, PhD Candidate, 26 Years Old, TPS Holder

> *You know, it's not very easy as a Black person in white dominated field, or in the school, to already feel alone and then putting that factor of being undocumented forward. It can be very isolating and very lonely and it's just hard. Very hard.*

Lucy was another powerful participant. She was the only TPS holder I interviewed and the only person from Haiti. She shared a unique perspective that I had never considered that her proximity to Florida made her even more of a target for deportation. I remember during the interview she told me that Haitians were the cheapest to deport and that was horrifying for her because she resided in Florida. However, Lucy was firm in her plans to enter the medical field even as an undocumented person. Lucy wanted us to know that while it is difficult to be an undocumented person, it is even lonelier to be an undocuBlack person.

Teresa, Current College Student, 26 Years Old, DACA Recipient

With both identities, there's just so many battles that you have to overcome and fight through. With being Black, the oppression and the systemic racism, it's just hard sometimes to even balance both or balance the issues. Sometimes, I also feel that it sucks being directly impacted by legislation; it feels like you're moved around like a game piece or something.

Teresa had a gritty story. She struggled with her mental health and did not have access to the information or resources she needed as a young teenager. As a result of lack of resources, she has been navigating college for over six years. At the time of the interview, Teresa had finally found a balance to her college journey and felt hopeful about the future. She wanted us to know that undocuBlack people were directly impacted by trauma, depression, systemic racism, legislation, and further marginalization from the undocumented community. Teresa's story shows us that we need to advocate for mental health resources for the undocumented community.

Mitch, College Student, 20 Years Old, Undocumented

I feel good because I am at HBCU. I feel alone as an undocumented person. Lots of restrictions. I want a car and to move freely around.

Mitch was one of the younger participants, and he was optimistic about his future, even as an undocumented person without any legal status. His spirit was contagious. Mitch was also unique in that he came to America when he was 17 years old, so he did not get to experience much of the K-12 experience. Additionally, he felt fortunate to attend an HBCU because he was validated in his racial experience. For Mitch, attending an HBCU created a safe space for him because he was surrounded by Black people. Furthermore, Mitch also had access to TheDream.US[1] scholarship, which covered tuition, room, and board – this released some of the traditional burden that other undocumented students face; the scholarship gave him freedom to focus on school. He wanted us to know that being undocumented is limiting and that HBCUs[2] are good spaces for undocuBlack people.

Taryn, College Graduate, 24 Years Old, DACA Recipient

> *I feel like honestly if I wasn't undocumented, I would have been more open to having friends in college. I probably would have pursued things that I would dream about. I was robbed of my college experience because I was not able to do spring breaks and things like that.*

Taryn struggled with building and maintaining relationships in college because of her undocumented status. She was a commuter student and rarely found time to nurture relationships. Taryn was vulnerable in sharing her experiences with me, and she was particularly grateful that I was an undocuBlack person. She shared that her legal status limited her options and contributed to her not chasing after some of her dreams. The main insight Taryn wanted us to know was that her undocumented status limited her pursuit of opportunities and relationships.

Shannon, Recent College Graduate, 23 Years Old, Undocumented

> *I think, for me, in terms of college experience, I avoided any police encounters, but I think the biggest thing that happened on campus that really made me be like oh my God what does it mean to be undocuBlack and like what does this mean for me is that an alumni who was 1st gen and Kenyan got mistakenly arrested on campus due to a protest. As a result, it made me evaluate what would have happened to me if I got arrested without ID. It made me very terrified that I always need to have my ID on me. Also, I don't have DACA, so there's no protection whatsoever.*

Shannon was vibrant. She was an advocate for her community and felt particularly tasked with the goal of championing for those without DACA status. She navigated college without DACA, which created additional adversities for her as she traversed through higher education. However, while she struggled being the only undocuBlack person in undocumented spaces, she never let that deter her from showing up. She wanted us to know that there is no protection or opportunities for those without DACA status. As educators, we must continue to find ways to support those without DACA, as they, too, need champions.

Greg, College Graduate, 23 Years Old, DACA Recipient

America needs to fix their immigration system or they will continue to lose brilliant people like myself. Also, corporate America needs to do a better job of getting people from all cultures.

Greg was self-assured and hopeful. He was very confident in his skills and knew he contributed greatly to the American economy, his local community, and the overall fabric of the United States. He wanted us to know that he was not afraid to take his talents elsewhere.

Rosemary, Recent College Graduate, PhD Candidate, 22 Years Old, Undocumented

There's a push to include minorities in STEM, and I'd be eligible because I'm Black, but then ineligible because I'm not a citizen. Being undocumented has been more of a hindrance to me than being Black. I'll give you an example – during last summer, when all the riots were happening, I considered going out to the protests. But, I was like, I can't go because if I get caught up, we're in a different situation. I'm not just gonna get locked up, I will get deported. The other thing that comes to mind is dating. It is hard to date because I don't want anyone thinking I am trying to use them.

Rosemary was brilliant. She was also from Jamaica, which gave us an instant connection. Rosemary told her story from a perspective of fear because that's how she was taught to think of her precarious position as an undocuBlack person. She had no community, and her parents could not financially or emotionally support her collegiate dreams. Therefore, she navigated her college journey without much support or access to resources. She wanted us to know undocuBlack people live in a precarious space of being Black and undocumented.

Anthony, College Student, 22 Years Old, Undocumented

I don't experience most of the racial incidents that Black people experience. So, I don't really have an experience when it comes to joining these two identities. All I know is just like I'm undocumented and I've just learned to just deal with that. But when it comes to being Black and undocumented, I don't feel like an extra weight. I just see it as, oh I'm Black, so what. So yeah, that's just my experience.

For Anthony, race was not a factor in his day-to-day life. In fact, he was unwavering in his belief that race was not a factor as it related to his undocumented experience. It was important to include Anthony's experience because it shows the diversity of the undocuBlack experience, which I think should prompt scholars to investigate the differences among the Black student experience. He wanted us to know that he is navigating his salient identities knowing that it is his reality.

Gabby, College Graduate, JD Candidate, 24 Years Old, Undocumented

> When I was applying to law school, scholarships that I came across were specifically for Hispanic undocumented people. I don't think I saw one that was Black undocumented or DACA specific.

Gabby was motivated to be as educated as she could be about immigration policies. Without access to DACA, she understood the limits placed on her employment opportunities. However, she felt that education was the one avenue that no one could take from her. What she wanted us to know was that even resources for undocumented people exclude undocuBlack people – a common experience of most of the participants in the current study. She wanted us to know that without DACA status, undocuBlack people are further isolated and marginalized.

Fatima, College Student, 21 Years Old, DACA Recipient

> Having both identities has gotten me in spaces that I didn't think I would've been in. Like, I don't think if I was legal I would've gotten a full scholarship to college. I don't think my race plays a factor, specifically in school. I think it's just the overarching you know, being an undocumented individual.

Fatima's experience was similar to Anthony's in that they were both adamant that race does not greatly affect their undocumented experience. This variance points to the diversity of the undocuBlack experience. Fatima saw her undocumented status and her Blackness as super powers, a concept I really enjoyed learning more about. However, Fatima had DACA status which opened many doors for her. She was also a student at an HBCU, so she was often surrounded by students who looked like her. Additionally, Fatima was a recipient of TheDream.US scholarship, which alleviated many financial pressures. Fatima traversed through college without some of the burdens that other participants in this study faced. She did not think that race affected her opportunities and believed her undocumented status opened up doors for her. She wanted us to know that both her undocumented status and her Blackness were super-powers that got her into spaces and opportunities that would otherwise be closed to her.

Arion, College Student, 28 Years Old, DACA Recipient

My college experience has been different. It was impacted by COVID, and COVID really played a huge role in my college experience. I graduate in May, so technically, I haven't spent that much time on campus – spending one year I counted in person, so I didn't really experience that much. I don't display my status to people, so they don't really see me as an immigrant, they just assume I am an African American. Race does come into play though. I work on campus and I have had experiences related to my race. For instance, I was outside of Starbucks for a promotional event and someone called cam-pus services to complain about the music I was playing because it was Hip Hop music. So, people don't treat me differently because of my immigration status, but they do treat me differently because of my race.

Arion's journey was arduous, but he was determined. He was also Jamaican. He spoke about the impact of the COVID-19 pandemic on his college experience, a factor that most of the participants did not mention. Addition-ally, he noted that if he did not disclose his status to others, they assumed he was African American. Therefore, he was notably treated differently because of his race but not status. He wanted us to know that his collegiate experi-ence was impacted by many factors, including racism and the COVID-19 pandemic.

Summary

The responses above demonstrate the heterogeneity of the undocuBlack ex-perience. Some of the participants saw their race as a bigger hindrance than others. Others saw their legal status as having the most dominant effects on their lives. However, one common thread remained true: the undocuB-lack participants saw themselves as being invisible within the undocumented community, the Black community, and within society as a whole. Therefore, it is essential that we amplify undocuBlack voices.

Amplifying UndocuBlack Voices

While the intention to amplify undocuBlack voices is rooted in inclusion, I understand that it can also seem divisive because there is an underlying and implicit suggestion to decenter other voices; yet the opposite is true.

The undocumented community as a whole faces destructive, legal, structural, and financial barriers to higher education and upward mobility in the United States. Additionally, Black undocumented people have been widely ignored within the broader narrative of immigration. Furthermore, they have been disproportionately affected by the criminal justice system and immigration policies. Therefore, the two realities are true. In amplifying undocuBlack voices, the goal is to include their stories in the narratives, to think about their experiences when we champion for policies, and to embrace this invisible group. So, I propose three ways to amplify undocuBlack immigrant voices:

1) *Expand the undocumented narrative to include undocuBlack voices by way of media, scholars, practitioners, and faculty,*
2) *Mainstream immigrant organizations should partner with undocuBlack organizations to challenge the homogeneity of the undocumented narrative,*
3) *Higher education institutions should work to create more inclusive spaces on college campuses for undocuBlack students.*

Amplifying UndocuBlack Narratives

The Media and the Undocumented Community Should Expand the Undocumented Narrative to Include UndocuBlack Voices

Expanding the narrative means diversifying the stories we tell, grounding stories from the lens of undocuBlack immigrants, and challenging the one-sided narrative about the undocumented community. In practice, this looks like the disruption of programming for Immigrant Heritage Month and Black History Month. Typically, during Immigrant Heritage Month, the language and the stories we see only represent the Latinx community; instead, we can tell more stories about the undocuBlack experience as well. Through stories, we humanize the undocumented community and show who they are and what they contribute to the economy, our communities, and the overall image of America. The stories we tell and the framing of those stories are impactful on policies and public opinion (Haynes et al., 2016; Newman et al., 2020; Wei et al., 2019). Therefore, broadening the narratives to include the undocuBlack population could provide more perspective about the community and the challenges they face. If the media intentionally includes stories about undocuBlack people, this will disrupt the binary lens through which immigration is viewed and understood.

Through the *media*, we have the power to influence federal- and state-level policies. Therefore, the media plays a huge role in redefining the immigrant narrative by simply including the voices of undocuBlack people.

One of the ways the media can do this is to tell stories about the diversity of the Black experience; the media can demonstrate the myriad of ways that Black immigrants and African Americans share different experiences. Again, while Black immigrants are recognized as African American as a result of race, they sometimes interpret that experience differently (Benson, 2006; Fries-Britt et al., 2014). Black immigrants who are born abroad do experience race differently. However, many of the Black immigrants that I interviewed grew up in America and understood race in similar ways that African Americans do. Therefore, the media can promote and share stories that distinguish those experiences to illustrate that ethnic identity and nationality might be more salient to the experience of some Black immigrants than race (Griffin et al., 2016; Portes & Rumbaut, 2006). According to Ogbu and Simons (1998), the Black immigrants who voluntarily migrated to the United States came here to improve their lives, and while they might share and understand the slavery ancestral history, they understand it differently. The Black experience is very diverse, and the media can identify ways to exemplify this.

Additionally, the media can promote narratives distinguishing the experiences of Latinx undocumented immigrants from the experiences of Black undocumented people. Even with a common immigration status, their experiences have nuances, and the media can promote stories to showcase the unique struggles. One of the ways they can do this is to show the disparities with deportations for undocuBlack immigrants and other immigrant groups. Stories highlighting the inequalities experienced by different immigrant groups, specifically Black immigrants, can urge policymakers to examine immigration policies. Highlighting these types of stories can also influence the undocumented community to advocate for undocuBlack immigrants.

The *undocumented higher education community* plays a huge role in expanding the immigrant narrative as well. The scholars, practitioners, and faculty who interact with or work to create better experiences for all undocumented students on college campuses can help shift the narrative. At the collegiate level, this includes scaffolding of the research around Black Americans and undocuBlack students.

One way to expand the narrative is for *scholars* to differentiate between undocuBlack experiences on college campuses and the African American experience. This is important because scholars influence the policies and practices put in place by practitioners. Scholars and researchers conduct research and share their findings; those findings lead to institutional policy changes. Therefore, another way to expand the narratives is for the scholars to conduct research about the Black community to disaggregate these stories to reflect the diversity of the Black experience. This will lead to better resources and support for all types of Black students on campuses. For instance, Black immigrants who were raised abroad might need different spaces on college campuses than Black immigrants who grew up in America. This is also true for African American students; they too, might require different support at the institutional level. Therefore, it is a responsibility of the scholars to conduct and expand the narratives within the literature about the undocumented community and the Black community. Scholars have a responsibility to go beyond the Latinx perspective and dedicate time and resources to the undocuBlack student experience.

Another way to expand the narrative is for *practitioners* on college campuses to invite undocuBlack speakers to their campuses, undocumented student spaces, and policy discussions around how to serve the undocumented community. From my conversations with the undocuBlack participants, and drawing on my own personal experience, whenever undocuBlack participants shared spaces with the undocumented students, they never saw themselves represented in the programming. There were never speakers who were Black. The study abroad opportunities were never centered in African or Black countries, only Hispanic origin countries. UndocuBlack students wanted to hear from others who have experiences similar to them. Practitioners have a role to play in expanding the narrative by ensuring that their programming is inclusive and goes beyond the Latinx lens.

Faculty also plays a role in expanding the immigrant narrative. Students from my study often noted that faculty would be surprised that they were undocumented. They described their experiences in the classrooms, noting that faculty would often choose readings that were based only on the Latinx experience. Faculty have a duty to diversify the readings they assign in class when discussing the undocumented community. They should aim to spotlight and include research on the undocuBlack experience. While not many scholars are doing work about the undocuBlack experience, they do exist (see Hall, 2022; Palmer, 2017; Russell, 2022). Additionally, there are also scholars doing work about Black immigrants and Black international students, which is adjacent to learning about the undocuBlack experience (see Constantine et al., 2005; Fries-Britt et al., 2014; Kent, 2007; Mwangi, 2016; Mori, 2000). Faculty play a huge role in expanding the narrative as well.

It is my belief that by expanding the narratives, we gain a better understanding of the diversity of the undocumented community, we begin to fill the gaps in the literature, shed light on the disparities within the legal system, and we show the resiliency of this group.

Mainstream Immigrant Organizations Should Partner With UndocuBlack Organizations to Challenge the Homogeneity of the Undocumented Narrative

This amplification is through collaboration, including partnerships with organizations like the UndocuBlack Network, Black Alliance for Just Immigration (BAJI), and African Communities Together (ACT). Cross collaboration is important to amplify the undocuBlack experience because this will provide undocumented students with the ability to access information from different sources. Collaboration also leads to the recognition of the work that Black organizations are doing.

One of the first organizations that mainstream organizations like Immigrants Rising, United We Dream, The Presidents' Alliance on Higher Education and Immigration, FWD.us, National Immigration Law Center (NILC), and others should partner with is the *UndocuBlack Network (UBN)*.[3] As mentioned in earlier chapters, the UndocuBlack Network is an organization of undocumented and formerly undocumented people who work to support the undocuBlack community. The UndocuBlack Network was founded in 2016 as a group of people joined together to discuss the fate of the undocuBlack community. The UndocuBlack Network's vision is centered around resources for those who are undocuBlack, legislative advocacy that aims to center the Black community, and providing access to mental health support for the undocuBlack community.[4]

Partnering with an organization like UBN promotes the image that the undocumented community is diverse and there are resources specific for undocuBlack students. The UndocuBlack Network was a main source of comfort for some of the participants within the current study. However, many of the students within the current study simply did not know where to go for support, but with mainstream organizations highlighting and collaborating with UBN, they can steer undocuBlack students to a community that was designed with them in mind.

Mainstream organizations can collaborate with this organization through programming such as hosting events and workshops. With collaborations centered around events, others will know more about the UndocuBlack Network (UBN). Another way to collaborate with the UBN is through organizing policies. Additionally, mainstream organizations can partner with UBN to develop guides on how to work with those in the undocuBlack community. Finally, when mainstream organizations partner with an organization such as the UBN, they bring intentional visibility to the undocuBlack community.[5]

Another organization to partner with is *Black Alliance for Just Immigration* (BAJI). BAJI works to 'educate and engage African American and

Black immigrant communities to organize and advocate for racial, social and economic justice'.[6] At the core of their work, they

> [B]uild coalitions and initiate campaigns among communities to push for racial justice. At the local and regional level, BAJI provides training and technical assistance to partner organizations to develop leadership skills, works with faith communities to harness their prophetic voice, and initiates vibrant dialogues with African Americans and Black immigrants to discover more about race, our diverse identities, racism, migration and globalization.[7]

BAJI's work is essential because the aim is to bridge the gap with the African American community and the Black immigrant community. This work is central to supporting undocuBlack people because as noted in the current study, participants struggled with belonging in Black campuses spaces because the spaces only catered to the African American experience.

BAJI is doing impactful work within the immigrant space as they have published reports, tool kits, and webinars. One of their more prominent reports is *The State of Black Immigrants*[8] published in 2018, which provides a statistical portrait of Black Immigrants in the United States and the over-criminalization they face within the criminalization system. Another poignant report they released is *Black Lives at the Border* (Adossi et al., 2018),[9] which provides an account of Black migrant stories at the border and details enforcement on Black migrant communities. Among other notable reports are *Uncovering the Truth* (2023), which depicts violence and abuse against Black Migrants in detention centers, and *There is a Target on Us (2021)*, which details the impact of anti-Black racism on African Migrants at Mexico's Southern Border. Beyond the research-oriented reports, BAJI is dedicated to the visibility of the undocuBlack community.[10]

Another organization to engage with is *African Communities Together* (ACT), which is 'an organization of African immigrants fighting for civil rights, opportunity, and a better life for families in the U.S. and worldwide'.[11] ACT is dedicated to the fight of African immigrants, which is also necessary because they focus on a specific group within the undocuBlack community. As noted from the current participants, those from African countries suggested they had a hard time connecting with Caribbean and Black Americans. Therefore, this ACT space provides a much-needed focus on a specific group.

Furthermore, ACT is working toward implementing a meaningful change through critical services that the African immigrant community needs, such as legal services, leaders to advocate on their behalf, and legislative change at all levels. By providing African immigrants with legal services, they can access information about their status, and they have an opportunity to be informed about their space in America. If undocuBlack people have access to legal services, they will be better informed. Additionally, by training leaders to be advocates, ACT is empowering the community. Finally, changes at the federal, state, and local levels are necessary for improving the lives of undocuBlack people. Therefore, the work ACT is doing is important to share on broader platforms that have a national reach.[12]

Partnering with undocuBlack organizations not only leads to collaboration but also provides insight into the issues that undocuBlack immigrants face. Partnering also promotes multiple diverse narratives. Through meaningful and intentional partnerships, information is disseminated through multiple sources, and different types of immigrants will have access to it. While I spotlighted three particular organizations, other Black organizations are doing monumental work to dismantle racist systems and working to create better opportunities for undocuBlack people.

Higher Education Institutions Should Work to Create More Inclusive Spaces on College Campuses for UndocuBlack Students

Creating inclusive spaces requires diversifying DREAM Centers or USRCs with diverse representation, multilayered resources, and expanding the events to reach a broader audience. USRC staff should reflect the diversity of the undocumented community; this includes hiring and training practitioners who are also Black and can speak to the Black immigrant experience. As noted many times within the current study, the undocuBlack students felt like outcasts whenever they were in undocumented spaces on college campuses. They did not see anyone who looked like them or shared their experiences. Therefore, USRCs can be more intentional about hiring undocuBlack staff within those centers. Some universities and colleges are yet to provide students with a physical space for undocumented students; those institutions should ensure that guest speakers, programming, scholarships, and opportunities are inclusive to undocuBlack students.

Another way to build more inclusive campuses for undocuBlack students is collaboration between Black cultural centers and undocumented student organizations. They should work together to highlight the diversity of the undocumented community. This type of collaboration will produce informed students, faculty, and staff who would then be more equipped to support undocuBlack students. Through cross student collaboration, the undocumented community will learn more about the experiences of Black students, and the Black students will gain a better understanding of the undocumented community. Oftentimes, student organizations on college campuses work in isolation, but collaboration among student organizations can promote a sense of belonging and community for students.

Black cultural centers on college campuses have a duty to demonstrate the differences among the Black community and hold spaces for the diversity within the Black community. Therefore, hosting events for Caribbean students, African students, and African Americans can promote inclusivity. It also advances learning for students. The burden is not just on the undocumented student community to create space for undocuBlack students but on the Black community as well. Black cultural centers can investigate their programming, events, scholarships, or gatherings and disrupt programming it by including undocuBlack performers, scholars, and formerly undocumented people.

The Challenge

Ultimately, the current study should initiate ongoing conversation among educators, policymakers, scholars, the undocumented community, and the Black community. Understanding the impact of invisibility and the lack of belonging for undocuBlack students at the collegiate level is necessary for future change at the state, federal, and institutional levels. This study alerts us to the diverse nature of the undocumented community, the unique challenges that undocumented Black students with intersecting identities face, and the delicacies of undocuBlack immigrants to exist in centralized African American spaces on college campuses.

I challenge higher education institutions, immigrant-led organizations, immigrant scholars, and policymakers to work to amplify undocuBlack voices. We can accomplish this by expanding the undocumented narrative to include undocuBlack voices through the media, collaborating with undocuBlack organizations to challenge the homogeneity of the undocumented narrative, and creating more inclusive spaces within higher education institutions for undocuBlack students. The work to amplify undocuBlack voices is not just the work of the undocumented and Black community, but it is also the work of the media, scholars, educators, practitioners, staff, and faculty.

Notes

1. All participants who had access to TheDream.US scholarship spoke highly of this opportunity. It is my hope that TheDream.US will continue to be diverse and intentional with the recipients of this award.
2. Another study I hope to conduct is to explore a sense of belonging at HBCUs for undocuBlack students.
3. This partnering is not to suggest that organizations such as UBN, BAJI, and ACT are not already powerhouses on their own. The goal is to promote collaboration.

4. For undocuBlack students reading this book and wanting to find community, the UndocuBlack Network has chapters in New York, Los Angeles, and Washington, DC. According to the UBN, the chapters are focused on providing safe spaces for undocuBlack people.
5. To learn more about how to partner or donate to UBN, email them at info@undocublack.org and visit their site: https://undocublack.org/ourwork
6. https://baji.org/
7. https://baji.org/
8. https://baji.org/wp-content/uploads/2020/03/sobi-fullreport-jan22.pdf
9. https://baji.org/wp-content/uploads/2020/03/black-lives-at-the-borderfinal-2.pdf
10. To learn more about BAJI, visit their site here: https://baji.org/
11. https://africans.us/what-we-do
12. To learn more about ACT, visit their site: https://africans.us/

References

Adossi, N., Belay, T., Lipscombe, C., & Ndugga-Kabuye, B. (2018). (rep.). *Black lives at the border: Black alliance for just immigration.*
Benson, J. (2006). Exploring the racial identities of Black immigrants in the United States. *Sociological Forum, 21*(2), 219–247. https://doi.org/10.1007/s11206-006-9013-7
Black Alliance for Just Immigration. BAJI. (n.d.). Retrieved from https://baji.org/.
Constantine, M., Anderson, G., Berkel, L., Caldwell, L., & Utsey, S. (2005). Examining the cultural adjustment experiences of African international college students: A qualitative analysis. *Journal of Counseling Psychology, 52*(1), 57–66. https://doi.org/10.1037/0022-0167.52.1.57
Fries-Britt, S., Mwangi, C., & Peralta, A. (2014). The acculturation experiences of Foreign-born students of color in physics. *Journal of Student Affairs Research and Practice, 51*(4), 459–471. https://doi.org/10.1515/jsarp-2014-0045
Goff, T., Mohamed, Z., Claude, R., Haba, M., Diaz, A., Lafortune, F., & Quirk, A. (2023). (rep.). *Uncovering the truth: Violence and abuse against Black migrants in immigration detention.* Black LGBTQIA+ Migrant Project (BLMP), Black Alliance for Just Immigration (BAJI), UndocuBlack Network, Freedom for Immigrants (FFI).
Griffin, K. A., Cunningham, E. L., & George Mwangi, C. A. (2016). Defining diversity: Ethnic differences in Black students' perceptions of racial climate. *Journal of Diversity in Higher Education, 9*(1), 34–49.
Hall, K. (2022). Undocumented Black students and hermeneutical injustice: Higher education's role in leaving them out of the undocumented conversation. *Journal of First-Generation Student Success, 2*(3), 143–160. https://doi.org/10.1080/26906015.2022.2115327
Haynes, C., Merolla, J., & Ramakrishnan, S. K. (2016). *Framing immigrants: News coverage, public opinion, and policy.* Russell Sage Foundation.
African Communities Together. (n.d.). Retrieved from https://africans.us/.
Kent, M. M. (2007). Immigration and America's Black population. *Population Reference Bureau, 62*(4), 3–16.
Mori, S. (2000). Addressing the mental health concerns of international students. *Journal of Counseling & Development, 78*, 137–144.
Morley, S. P. (2021). (rep.). *There is a target on us.* Black Alliance for Just Immigration. Retrieved from https://baji.org/wp-content/uploads/2021/01/The-Impact-of-Anti-Black-Racism-on-African-Migrants-at-Mexico.pdf.

Mwangi, C. (2016). Exploring a sense of belonging among Black international students at an HBCU. *Journal of International Students, 6*(4).

Newman, B., Merolla, J. L., Shah, S., Lemi, D. C., Collingwood, L., & Ramakrishnan, S. K. (2020). The Trump effect: An experimental investigation of the emboldening effect of racially inflammatory elite communication. *British Journal of Political Science, 51*(3), 1138–1159. https://doi.org/10.1017/S0007123419000590

Ogbu, J. U., & Simons, H. D. (1998). Voluntary and involuntary minorities: A cultural-ecological theory of school performance with some implications for Education. *Interdisciplinary Perspectives on the New Immigration*, 1–34. https://doi.org/10.4324/9781315054216-1

Palmer, B. J. (2017). The crossroads: Being black, immigrant, and undocumented in the era of #BlackLivesMatter. *Georgetown Journal of Law & Modern Critical Race Perspectives, 9*(1), 99–121.

Portes, A., & Rumbaut, R. G. (2006). *Immigrant America: A portrait.* University of California Press.

Russell, F. (2022). *The invisibility of undocuBlack students within the undocumented community in higher education* [Doctoral dissertation, Temple University]. Theses and Dissertations. https://doi.org/10.34944/dspace/7734

UndocublackNetwork. UndocuBlack Network. (n.d.). Retrieved from https://undocublack.org/.

Wei, K., Booth, J., & Fusco, R. (2019). Cognitive and emotional outcomes of Latino threat narratives in news media: An exploratory study. *Journal of the Society for Social Work and Research, 10*(2), 213–236. https://doi.org/10.1086/703265

INDEX

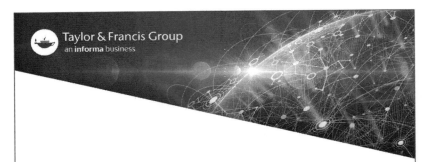